596 SWITCH

THE IMPROBABLE JOURNEY FROM THE PALOUSE TO PASADENA

RYAN D. LEAF

GREG WITTER

FOREWORD BY MIKE PRICE

ISBN 978-0-9829505-3-1

Crimson Oak Publishing, LLC
840 Bishop Blvd. Suite 200
Pullman, Wa 99163
Visit our website at www.CrimsonOakPublishing.com

Crimson Oak Publishing books are available at special discounts when purchased
in bulk for premiums, sales promotions as well as for fund raising. Special editions
including personalized covers, excerpts and corporate imprints can be created in large
quantities for special needs. For details contact the Special Sales Director at the address
above or send an e-mail to specialmarkets@crimsonoakpublishing.com

Printed in the United States of America
First Printing October, 2011
10 9 8 7 6 5 4 3 2 1

CONTENTS

THANK YOU

Thank you Lord for my family, John my father, Marcia my mother, Jeffrey my brother, and Brady my baby bro.

It's us five against the world we've decided and if it weren't for you I would not be the son, brother, and man I'm becoming.

I played football for the enjoyment and competition, but I'd be lying if I didn't say I didn't play for you four and the way you looked at me when I walked off that field, seeing the pride and tears in your eyes.

Those four years in Pullman brought a family together like no other and I'm thankful for every moment we got to experience together, I'll never forget a minute of it.

This is dedicated to my family and the amazing support you've been to me my entire life.

I LOVE YOU
Go Cougs,

Ryan D. Leaf

FOREWORD
Mike Price

Did Ryan Leaf tell you what was on his mind? Yes he did. Did Ryan Leaf wear his emotions on his sleeve? Many times. Was Ryan Leaf immature in his younger days? Absolutely. And for that he gets a bad rap. I read stories and personally see some of the real bad acting that goes on in the sports world and I scratch my head why people around the nation have for years looked at Ryan with fire in their eyes.

Let me tell you about Ryan Leaf. If life's dealt you a blow, he'll be the first one not just on the phone, but on your doorstep, offering moral support. If you want to see loyalty in action, take a look at the lifelong bonds Ryan has developed with people at every stage of his life. Ryan is not just a good guy, he's a great guy. After he signed his contract with the Chargers, one of the first things he did was write a big check to WSU, and then he bought new uniforms for his high school. He views his family as the greatest gift he's ever received. He'll sign autographs until every last kid is taken care of. There are people all over the sports world who are held up as heroes and they're very far from being heroes. They don't hold a candle to Ryan Leaf.

With Ryan, I always liked the analogy of the thoroughbred race horse. Have you ever seen a thoroughbred getting into the gate? They can be a little feisty at times. They're wired that way, and it's part of what makes them so special. Now, who would you rather have leading your team on the field, a plow horse or a thoroughbred? Ryan was a thoroughbred.

The story he tells in this book is equal parts entertaining, fascinating, and heartwarming. It's a coming-of age-story about a group of young men who worked tirelessly to accomplish something that hadn't been done in nearly 70 years. He brings people to life in these pages, providing background and context and perspective that captures the magic of a very special time and place. It's a wonderful story. More than anything, my hope is that all who read it will come to appreciate the real Ryan Leaf – a young man of character and strength – who I'm proud to call one of the finest people I know.

MIKE PRICE
Washington State Head Coach, 1989-2002

IT'S TOUGH TO DEFEND

"Not often, but every now and then, Ryan Leaf's thoughts drift to the twilight of a sunny day near the San Gabriel Mountains. He thinks of the final two seconds inexplicably taken off the Rose Bowl clock – two seconds that could have meant football immortality for Leaf and his fellow Cougars but instead handed Michigan a national championship. The play WSU was going to run was called 596 Switch."

Those words were written two years ago by a sportswriter named Barry Bolton, the only person who ever asked me what we were going to run if the clock hadn't hit zero on that first day of January in 1998.

We were 26 yards from victory with no timeouts left and 101,219 people on their feet, holding their breath. I had the option of spiking the ball to stop the clock or taking the snap and firing.

When I called Dick Burleson a dozen years after the fact, to get his view of the chaotic end, I was hoping to hear some regret, that in retrospect the clock shouldn't have been allowed to run down and that we should have been given a final shot. It wouldn't change anything, of course, but it would add to the legend of it all. Dick was the head official that day in Pasadena. It was his final game in stripes after a long and respected career calling games in the Southeast Conference. He speaks with a southern accent and is about as personable and charming as anyone can be.

"There is no doubt in my mind that it was the right call," he told me. "I knew it was going to be close, the ball and the clock, but when you spiked the ball, when the ball hit the ground, the game clock read double zero . . . The TV clock may not have said that, but the game clock did . . . I really don't think it's physically possible to complete that action in less than two seconds."

We didn't see it the same way then or now, but we did agree on two things: That "it was an absolutely great football game" and I should have run a play at the end rather than spike the ball. In the moment, however, it seemed entirely reasonable to get set, wait for the restart whistle, snap the ball and spike it.

I don't know if 596 Switch subsequently would have worked, but I do know this: We had run it many times that season and the results were almost always positive. It's a tough play to defend, especially when you have five receivers as talented as ours were. Mike Price told reporters "I'm betting on Ryan Leaf completing the pass if given the chance." Whether he was being nice or really meant it, I just wanted the opportunity.

Chris Jackson and Nian Taylor were going to run hitches on the outside to freeze the cornerbacks so Shawn Tims and Shawn

McWashington would have space on corner routes to the end zone. Kevin McKennzie would have been headed down the middle on a post pattern.

Coach Price had had 596 Switch in his playbook as long as he could remember, and it's still there to this day. The beauty in it is the switch. Normally, McKenzie would run the corner route and McWashington the post. On this one, they swap roles, which hopefully would cause split-second confusion in the defense. On a football field, you can move mountains in a split second. The other beautiful thing about the play is that the safety on that side of the field – the right side – would have both those receivers coming directly at him and then he'd have to choose one – and only one – to cover out of the break: Shawn going to the corner or Kevin going to the post.

There are a lot of moving parts on a football field and any one of them can make or break any given play. If the Michigan middle linebacker dropped deep to take away the post, the play would have been in serious trouble. If not, maybe there's a bronze statue of Kevin – dancing into the Rose Bowl end zone – planted outside Martin Stadium right now.

"What if WSU had 2 more seconds?" asked Seattle Times columnist Steve Kelley the next day. "One more play. A game this intense and delicious deserved it," he said. "One more second. One Mississippi. One last chance at a miracle."

So close and yet so far. The name of the play proved ironic. The course of destiny, it seemed, was replaced – switched – by the clock. That, in turn, ended a magical, almost fairy tale-like run to national prominence. And personally, there was another switch amid it all. Unbeknownst to me or anyone else at the time, my ascension as a football player effectively came to a halt as the clock ran out that day.

What might have been?

It's a question that hangs over the 84th Rose Bowl game because of the controversial end. It's a question that hangs over my pro career because of the controversial beginning.

But there's another metaphor to be found in the name of the play – 596 Switch – that resonates so much louder than any other. The 1997 Washington State Cougars pulled an end run on doubters near and far. "Washington State can't compete with USC and UCLA," they had said for years. "Washington State can't out-recruit Washington," they insisted. "Washington State can't aspire to more than minor bowl games," they believed. "Washington State doesn't have the depth to compete over the course of an entire season," they claimed.

We proved them wrong. We ran a figurative 596 Switch, going directly at them with our resourcefulness, spirit and determination. Who were they going to cover coming out of the break, the intellectual kid from Seattle running the corner route, the up-from-the-bootstraps kid running the post, or maybe one of the decoys waiting in the weeds? We turned old perceptions on their head. We switched fields on the Pac-10 and the nation, uniting a community and fueling the idea that teamwork, dreams and hard work can overcome outdated opinions and negative thinking.

It had been four years to the day since I decided to become a Cougar. Four years since Mike Price told me we would go to the Rose Bowl together. Four years of ups and downs and lessons to last a lifetime. The journey to this place was even more remarkable than I had dreamed it would be that winter day in Great Falls when I first started to believe.

WHY IS THIS ALL HAPPENING?

I knew it was a bad idea and my clammy palms were telling me as much. It was February of 2010, and a typical winter night of cold and drizzle in Seattle. As I walked into the Westin for the annual dinner celebrating Washington State's newest class of recruits, I really, truly had an urge to turn around and go home. I hadn't been to a WSU event like this in over a decade. The public meltdown of my pro career left me embarrassed to be around Cougars because I felt I had let them down. To make matters worse, my addiction to prescription painkillers, when I was coaching at West Texas A&M, had been all over the news in the last year.

"Cougs are a very forgiving bunch," Jack Thompson, the legendary WSU quarterback, told me. He was one of the people who convinced me to come to the dinner. Jack is someone I admire immensely. He's smart, caring, a great family man, and probably the best goodwill ambassador WSU has ever had. When Jack talks, I listen. But now that the day for the dinner had arrived, I was wishing I hadn't. What would people think when they saw me?

A lot had happened since I was on top of the Cougar world at the 1998 Rose Bowl. Now it was a dozen years later, and I wondered if people would even want to say hello. Would there be sideways glances? Whispers?

There was a social hour before the dinner and I made sure I stayed close to Jack and other folks I knew pretty well. Hanging out in the crowded foyer seemed safe. Going into the ballroom with 400 or 500 people you had let down was risky. So I stayed in the foyer as long as I could, long after Jack and the rest went inside. Ian Furness, the outstanding Seattle radio commentator, was the emcee that night. Once his formal spiel was underway, I figured I'd head inside. Everyone would be focused on Ian, so I could just find my seat and be safe for the night. I wasn't even halfway to my table when Ian said, ". . . and the next person I'd like to introduce is just now walking in – right over there . . ." He pointed my way. " . . . our quarterback, our Rose Bowl quarterback – Ryan Leaf."

As the spotlight swung in my direction, I froze and then sheepishly waved my arm, hoping there wouldn't be any muffles of "What the hell is he doing here?" Dead silence probably would have been worse than anything. But people clapped, and it was like a weight being lifted from my shoulders. As Ian said a few nice things about me, the clapping grew louder. I started to navigate toward my seat and the spotlight followed and the applause grew louder. My eyes started to well up. And then everyone was on their feet cheering.

Never in my life have I fought so hard to fight back tears. Jack was right – Cougars are a very forgiving bunch. If someone had asked me to say anything at that moment, I don't think I could have even uttered my name. I was really choked up. This was like a dream. *How did I get here? Why was this happening?* I was surrounded by successful businessmen and women, plus some of the greatest names ever in Cougar football, and I was receiving an ovation. Ryan Leaf, the NFL bust. Ryan Leaf, the PR train wreck. Ryan Leaf, the cocky jerk. Implausible, surreal, I'm not sure what adjective to place on it all but I was overwhelmed. And then there was clarity – a calm clarity that came over me and transported me back to Pullman so many years ago. The people, the spirit, the culture. The memories of four special years were racing through my mind. Keith Jackson once said of WSU, "The place gets in your blood and you never let go." He was right.

The thoughts, memories and emotions of four unforgettable years in Pullman poured over me. I stood there in amazement. All these people were applauding me, but I should have been applauding them for staying in my corner all these years. The room quieted down and I spent much of the next two hours in a blissful daze. I wanted to call my mom and dad and tell them this turned out to be a night I'd never forget. I spent the rest of the evening talking with, but mostly listening to, Cougar fans. They shared their stories about games we had in common. And it was eye-opening to me. I had experienced it all from the field, sidelines and locker room. They had experienced it from the stands, from their living rooms and from their favorite bars. This was like one of those movies where they play the same scene over and over but from the vantage point of different characters, so your perspective changes and grows. People would tell me what they were doing, the friends they were with and the pride they felt when Leon Bender and the Cougar defense held UCLA at the goal line, when Shawn McWashington leveled the block and Kevin McKenzie scored at USC, when Steve Gleason de-cleated Cam Cleland in the Apple Cup, when the Cougs came running out of the tunnel before the start of the Rose Bowl, and on and on. My Cougar teammates and I had created an indelible, joyous mark in the hearts and minds of so many people. I just didn't realize it at the time. And now, all these years later, the stories were like a warm blanket being draped over my shoulders.

One would have to know my story to fully understand what an amazing gesture that evening was to me and why it meant so much at that point in my life. But this wasn't about me. It was about the Cougar Nation. This was about the people who made, and make, WSU such a special place. This was a statement about shared experiences, loyalty and friendship. Being a Cougar means you're part of a family. Walk down any street in America with a WSU t-shirt or hat on and at some point in your day someone's going to say "Go Cougs!" to you. There's a bond that is unlike any other. Being a Husky, Duck, or Trojan just doesn't carry the same level of spirit and caring. I made a decision when I was 17 years old to attend Washington State. At that time I had no idea what a monumental decision it truly was. It was a decision that would shape me – and embrace me – for the rest of my life. The saying goes, "Once a Coug, Always a Coug." There are as many examples of the meaning of that phrase as there are Cougars. You're about to read mine, and the life lessons of loyalty, love and persistence that come with it.

THE BEGINNING

Once upon a time there was this 17-year-old kid who grew up in a pretty standard middle-class family in a middle-class neighborhood. Mom was a nurse and dad was in insurance. There were three kids, all boys, and the oldest one, the 17-year-old, came across so cocky to outsiders that they'd have never guessed he was actually a terribly insecure young man. He was also a pretty good athlete. So when colleges started calling and writing, some of the smaller ones inviting him to play basketball and the bigger ones selling football, he jumped in head first. He was going to be the next Terry Bradshaw. That was his goal since childhood. And now all these coaches were telling him it was not only possible, but maybe even destined. The confidence factor reached new heights at the same time the insecurity was burning underneath.

The result was a very confused kid named Ryan Leaf. Talking about it now, so many years later, feels a bit like I'm a third-party retracing someone else's journey. But that was me and the journey was mine.

I was good at two things, athletics and lying. I was always worried about what others were thinking about me or how I was being perceived. I was always very aware of what others were saying about me and, if I didn't like it, I did something about it, usually to the chagrin of my parents, particularly my mother. Soon lying, to make the story more about who I wanted people to think I was, ultimately won out. I tried to gain control of who I really was for years. This is that story.

While the years have thickened my skin, softened my temper and expanded my perspectives, one thing has not changed since those days as a teenager in Great Falls: the focus. I had, and have, an ability to focus intensely on things that are important to me. In those days, my aim was to be successful in sports – no matter what. Genetically speaking, running, jumping and throwing were more than natural for me. They were like electric bolts charging my body. Add in a tunnel-vision mindset and the makings are there to rule the court or field. While great for winning games, this limited me socially. To say I was competitive is an understatement. I was hyper-competitive, to the point that my mom started to get concerned about it when I was around 9 or 10 because I was alienating all the kids my age. I had to beat them in everything, every time. I had to. This extremism pushed people away and rarely allowed me to establish friendships and relationships outside the realm of team sports. I told myself that in order to be understood and to fit in, I needed to get out of Montana and find a bigger pool to swim in. That thinking, of course, was delusional. But it put me on a path that ultimately led to the highest highs of the Pac-10 Conference, as well as the lowest lows of the NFL.

People make decisions about where to go to college in many different ways. Maybe it's following in the footsteps of parents. Maybe it's financial considerations. Or interest in a particular major. In my case, it was mostly about athletics – playing early, getting the right coaching and then high-stepping into the NFL. I knew very little about Washington State University. Growing up in Montana, it was all Montana State – where my dad went to school – and Montana. My first introduction to Wazzu was a letter that arrived in the mail in August of 1993, just before my senior year at C.M. Russell High. It had come in a round-about kind of way. I had attended a football camp earlier that summer in California and one of my fellow campers was the son of then-WSU athletic director Jim Livengood. Jim and my parents started talking during one of the sessions and, just like that, I was suddenly on the Cougars' recruiting radar. As I recall, it was a standard recruiting letter, but it prompted me to do a little research beyond what little I already knew about WSU – that Mark Rypien, a Super Bowl MVP, and Drew Bledsoe, the No. 1 pick in the most recent NFL draft, went there.

What I learned about WSU, I liked. It had great school spirit, a family-type atmosphere, one of the best schools in the nation for what I was interested in studying (broadcast communications), and a head coach known for mentoring quarterbacks. So one Friday in September, right after one of my high school games ended, my dad and I took off for Pullman. We stayed overnight in Missoula at my Aunt Jackie and Uncle Charlie's house and then got up at the crack of dawn to drive over the mountains, through Idaho and into

Washington. Total drive time was about eight hours. This was an unofficial visit, nothing formal. I remember driving through the rolling wheat fields between Spokane and Pullman and wondering where the hell this place was. As we took that left turn off Highway 195, moving slowly in the long line of game-day traffic, and came up over the final hill, I got my first glimpse of what would ultimately be my home for the next four years. It was a gorgeous day. Off in the distance, soaking in the sun and sitting on a hill with nothing but blue skies in the background, was a set from a movie. Or so it seemed. Red brick buildings, a giant clock tower and lots of trees. All sitting on a hill. It was like an oasis in a sea of wheat.

We found Martin Stadium pretty easily because it sits squarely in the middle of campus. I bet there's not another school in the country with their football stadium sitting right in the middle of everything. I thought that was the coolest thing. We sat just below the press box and I remember watching warm ups and being shocked at how big all the quarterbacks were. The Cougars dismantled Oregon State that day, 51-6. Singor Mobley was a wrecking ball on defense and Deron Pointer was the man on offense, catching two TD passes and returning a kickoff past midfield. Best of all, quarterback Mike Pattinson threw the ball 41 times. Forty-one times! That stat alone was enough to get me fired up about WSU. I briefly met some of the Cougar coaches afterward, but Mike Price wasn't one of them. He was moving fast, and just gave me a smile and wave as he motored down a hallway. As my father and I headed back to the mountain passes and home I thought Pullman seemed like a great place. But I was far, far from being sold. Plus, I didn't have an actual scholarship offer in hand yet. Today, in this era of earlier and earlier offers and commitments, it would be insane to wait until fall to make an offer to one of your top QB targets, but in those days the senior season of high school still was critical in the assessment process.

As my senior season at C.M. Russell wound down, I narrowed my list of college possibilities to Washington State, Miami, Colorado State, Colorado, Oregon and UCLA. Subconsciously, the fact I was from Montana played a big role in shaping that list – something that didn't occur to me until years later, and now makes me smile. WSU's point man in recruiting me was offensive line coach John McDonell, who had been an NAIA All-American at Carroll College in Helena and later was the head coach at Scobey High in the northeast corner of the state. Miami was coached by Dennis Erickson, who had played and coached at Montana State and also coached high school ball in Billings. One of his assistants helping recruit me was former Montana State head coach Dave Arnold. Colorado State, meanwhile, was coached by Sonny Lubick, a Butte native and former Montana State player and assistant. And Colorado had Jon Knutson on their side. Jon was a star senior at C.M. Russell when I was a freshman and I idolized him. He was a junior linebacker for the Buffs and involved in recruiting me there.

It never dawned on me at the time that these schools were playing the "Montana card." I just figured Montanans were everywhere. Recruiting is a very odd process: grown men chasing a bunch of 17- and 18-year-olds who think they're hot stuff. Livelihoods depend on how well you woo these kids, so coaches have to find and use every possible tool to help get the guys they want. Being recruited can be intoxicating. You're wanted! You're loved! You're adored! The best recruiters make you feel like you're the only one they want. For me, this was just fueling an ego that was already too big. And working the ol' Montana angle was smart. While I always wanted to leave home for school, the fact is that I was, and remain, very proud to be a Montanan. There's not that many of us – the elk, deer and antelope outnumber humans by a long shot – so we tend to consider ourselves among the lucky few. Waving the state flag clearly was the right thing for those schools to do in recruiting me because UCLA and Oregon were my only finalists without a home-state connection. UCLA was in the mix because their coach, Terry Donahue, was something of a star himself and the Bruins were really rockin' back then. I don't recall exactly why Oregon was on my list, but I presume it was because the assistant coach recruiting me, Mike Bellotti, seemed like a good guy.

It was a full 18 years before I learned that Coach McDonell – a.k.a. Coach Mac – wasn't a Montana native. He was born and raised in Spokane, for God sakes, yet in all my conversations with him all I ever heard about was Montana – college in Helena, coaching in Scobey, his cousins in Great Falls, and so on. Heck, the way he talked, I figured his family must have homesteaded the place shortly after Lewis and Clark came through. Whether Spokane or Helena, though, one thing was undeniable about Coach Mac: He's a gentle giant – a big man with a bigger heart. There was no way anyone wouldn't like WSU if he was the first impression – an opinion backed up by the fact he was also the lead recruiter for Drew Bledsoe four years earlier. Coach Mac and I kept in close contact that fall of 1993 and he came to watch our state semifinal playoff game against Missoula Big Sky. We lost a heartbreaker that day and I had two long TD runs – *two!* – that were called back because of inadvertent whistles. In early December he invited me to take an official visit to Pullman. This would be the first official visit I would make to a college. In most cases, recruits are given plane tickets to and from the university and you usually travel by yourself. But I wanted my dad to join me, so we drove to Pullman – 16 hours round trip – for the second time in three months. On the drive, I remember thinking Pullman was far enough from home to truly be going away to school but close enough to get back to my Montana mountains and rivers.

The visit started Friday evening with introductions to all of the coaching staff. I think back and try to remember some telling, ground-breaking moment in that initial handshake with Mike Price but my mind always takes me first to Chad DeGrenier. He was my host for the weekend, a fellow quarterback who had transferred in from a junior college and wound up starting a couple games that season after Mike Pattinson had broken his collar bone. Chad was a super nice guy and a devout Christian. He had been picked to be my host because the coaches somehow had the impression that I, too, was deeply religious and wouldn't be up for going out to parties. To this day, I don't know why the coaches thought that. Not that I have anything against religion, but I'm not exactly a holy roller. I didn't drink while I was in high school and my family and I went to church every Sunday – I was even an altar boy at St. Luke's Catholic Church – so that may have led to their erroneous conclusions. As a result, my first night on a college campus was less than wild and crazy.

THE BEGINNING

We started out at Coach Price's home for a dinner party with all the other recruits and their hosts. I must have been bug-eyed, because the basement was like walking into a wing of the hall of fame. It was full of memorabilia, from bowl trophies to framed jerseys of Drew Bledsoe, Timm Rosenbach and others. It was awe-inspiring to see autographed pictures of Bledsoe standing alongside the man who could be my future coach. The food was amazing, too – steaks the size of dinner plates and all the fixings to go along. I was so impressed by all this, and of course focused only on myself, that I can't even remember what other recruits were there with me.

After dinner, the evening was open for free time, and Chad proceeded to take me on a tour of campus and then over to Moscow to see the Idaho campus. Lots of driving around, lots of sights, but not much fun. *Is this it? Is this all that college is cracked up to be?* When he was dropping me off at the hotel, I couldn't contain myself. "What the hell? Aren't you going to take me to a party or something?" He looked at me in astonishment. He said he'd been told by the coaches that I wasn't into the party scene. "Hey, if I'm going to be here for the next five years, I want to know what this is going to all be about," I said. Chad actually looked relieved and told me he'd have a party plan for the next day.

The sun was out the next morning and it was one of those stunning Palouse days. Academic meetings and tours dominated the first half of the day but then we went over to Martin Stadium. I had been there in September for the game with Oregon State, but with no one inside it looked massive to me. The idea of playing here gave me goose-bumps. A few guys were on the field throwing and catching and I was once again struck by their size and athleticism. That evening, the coaches brought us to the locker room and we found jerseys lying side-by-side on the floor in front of the lockers. There was No. 16 with LEAF on the back. I picked it up and looked at it and just smiled from ear to ear. I walked out of that locker room on cloud nine.

From there, as promised, Chad DeGrenier took me out to party. After a quick stop for a burger at a place I would later come to love – the Cougar Country Drive-in – we met up with two very large guys named Ryan McShane and Jason McEndoo. They were both 6-6 and in the process of morphing from about 250 to 300 pounds or more. They were both freshmen offensive linemen who had just redshirted. These two were pieces of work. Ryan's nickname was Chop, presumably for his blocking skills, and Jason's was simply Mackey. They had already become the best of friends and were wild men to say the least. In the coming years, when an offensive lineman said, "Let's go have a few beers," I knew the actual meaning was "let's hit a party and down a keg." So when they said "let's go have a few beers," I took them literally. Soon we were walking into a house that Aaron Price lived in with some of his fraternity brothers. Aaron was the Cougars' senior placekicker – and Mike Price's son. But on this night, he was the maestro. The place was packed and the fun was flowing. I think my chin hit the ground when I spotted these beautiful co-eds who were dressed up as sexy Santa's elves. Oh man, this college life is something, I thought. You might think a cocky kid like me would just jump right into the middle of all this, but I felt so out of place and awkward that I just found a corner and tried to stay out of sight. What hit me most about it all was the freedom. These people were living the life every high school senior dreamed about.

Chad came over and asked how I was doing. He was like an older brother watching over me. He's really the type of guy every parent would want their son to turn out to be. It was no surprise later in life that Chad became a standout quarterback in the Arena Football League and a very successful high school coach in Arizona. I couldn't have asked for a better host. And like Chad, I didn't have a single thing to drink that night. I was too scared. But as the night wore on and Chad introduced me around I started to loosen up. I got up enough nerve to try and talk to some of the girls at the party – even the scantily dressed elves. It must have been a comedy show for Chad, Chop, and Mack watching an awkward, gangly, 17-year-old try to say anything relevant to beautiful college girls. Big swings, and big misses definitely. With the football players, I think my swings were equally as big and off target as I regaled them with stories of my quarterbacking skills. Yeah, that was me, the egomaniac with a self-esteem problem. At some level, I think I acted so cocky in those days as a way of masking my insecurities and awkwardness in social settings.

Later that evening, Chad drove me and Chop and Mack back to their dorm, and as most nights ended after a night of drinking and running around, Chop and Mack proceeded to start some trouble with some fraternity guys and I got to witness my first college fight. It makes me laugh now, but it scared the hell out of me. These big linemen getting rowdy and boisterous and looking for trouble. Nothing really came of it, just some shit talking and posturing, but I could see how that all worked and how intimidating a football player could be on campus. We sat in Mack's room and talked about sports, school, girls, life and everything else.

He reminded me years and years later how I told him that I wore a wristband on my arm that had a 3 on it when I played basketball because that's all I did was hit three pointers. What an egotistical sucker I was.

Chad took me back to my hotel room around 4:00 in the morning and I lay in bed not able to fall asleep thinking about the night that had just transpired and what it all really meant. At 7:30 my short sleep came to an end. My dad was pounding on the door – we had to head over to Perkins for my exit interview with Coach Price and his staff. My father and I sat across from Coach as he extended me my first scholarship offer to play college football. I looked at my dad and didn't say a word, but he knew exactly what I was thinking – all those early mornings when he'd get up before work to play catch with me had paid off.

Coach Price would tell me years later that he didn't think my visit to WSU went well at all. My dad is a quiet, reserved, and introspective man who takes everything in, ponders it, and then makes good, correct decisions. Based on that, Coach Price concluded to his staff after breakfast, "We didn't get him!" Little did he know that Dad and I spoke almost all the way home that day about Pullman and our experience. I would take two more official visits – to Miami and Colorado State – before all was said and done, but my heart was definitely pointing toward WSU.

Ironically, the Cougar coaching staff's misguided idea that I was Mr. Religious actually made me like them all the more. They were just trying to respect what they thought my wishes were. It was so sincere and honest. This was the first of many pieces of evidence over the next four years that proved how special Mike Price and his staff were.

WHAT COULD HAVE BEEN

Shortly after my official trip to WSU, Dave Arnold, an assistant coach at Miami, came to Great Falls to visit with me and my parents. He of course was a Montana native - but not just any Montana native. He had been the head coach of the Montana State Bobcats in the 1980s, leading them to the 1984 Division I-AA national championship. My dad was an MSU graduate and, by extension, my brothers and I were all Bobcat fans. In our house, the name Dave Arnold meant something. That 1984 Bobcat team and their great quarterback, Kelly Bradley, are as vivid in my mind today as they were back then.

Coach Arnold's luster was bright before he arrived at our house that evening, but it reached blinding proportions the minute he stepped through the front door. That's because he was wearing the coolest ring I'd ever seen – a massive salute to the Miami Hurricanes' 1989 national championship. It was gold, with a giant emerald gem in the middle embedded with diamonds that formed a large numeral 1. The thing was like a spotlight in our living room, catching the light from every lamp and shooting beams through the house. Other than the fact he mentioned he had another ring at home for the Canes' 1991 national title, I don't remember much else we talked about, but I was impressed enough to tell him I'd take an official visit to the Coral Cables campus just before Christmas break.

This would be my third of the five official visits the NCAA allows prospective athletes to take. After visiting WSU, I had tripped to Colorado State. That one was a little awkward because I wasn't there on a weekend. In order to avoid conflicts with our basketball season at C.M. Russell, I hit Fort Collins on a Sunday, Monday and Tuesday. Sonny Lubick had just completed his first season as head coach of the Rams after previously serving as Coach Erickson's defensive coordinator at Miami. The offensive coordinator was Mick Dennehy. Both he and Coach Lubick were Butte natives and both had been head coaches in Montana early in their careers – Coach Lubick at Montana State and Coach Dennehy at Montana and Western Montana. The two of them were with me for what seemed like start to finish on my trip. They were incredibly likeable, and from the sounds of things they had a good plan to get CSU on the map. There was nothing fancy about this trip – a movie one night, a tour of the stadium, and lots of talking – but I left with a very positive impression. When I returned home I told Mom and Dad that I would get to play right away because their depth at quarterback was pretty thin. That was a huge selling point for me, and it thrust CSU right up the list with WSU. By the way, the plan that Coach Lubick told me about turned out to be as good as it sounded – he took the Rams to nine bowl games in his 15 seasons as head coach. The field at Hughes Stadium is now named in his honor.

As for Coach Arnold and the Hurricanes, I couldn't get that national championship ring of his out of my mind. Miami had won two of the last four national titles, and they had a passing guru for a head coach. They also had a long history of amazing quarterbacks, including the previous season's Heisman winner, Gino Torreta, a Heisman finalist a few years earlier in Steve Walsh, and three guys who were fixtures in the NFL –Jim Kelly, Bernie Kosar and Vinny Testaverde. Still, going to Miami was definitely a stretch for me. It was a long way from home in a city about as polar opposite from Great Falls as there is. I was really more curious than serious about going there, but since they were going to pay my way to check it out, I figured I had nothing to lose. Except maybe a little sleep. Getting to Miami from Great Falls was no easy feat. I had to change planes in Minneapolis and then Atlanta. I left Great Falls at the crack of dawn and arrived in Miami early that evening. As soon as I stepped off the plane I knew I was in a different world. I wasn't just a fish out of water, I was a fish outside my universe. It was warm and muggy – in December. I didn't know what to think of the Santa Claus in red shorts and tank top ringing the Salvation Army bell.

Coach Arnold was there to greet me and we headed straight to dinner at a posh restaurant on the water in South Beach. I wasn't dressed appropriately at all – jeans and a flannel shirt. I felt awkward and out of place and quickly realized how much more comfortable I was in Pullman and Fort Collins. The meal, however, improved my outlook. It was stone crab - mountains of stone crab that melted in my mouth. There were a couple other recruits on the trip. Like me, I think they were basketball players stuck doing the Sunday-through-Tuesday routine. My roommate was a guy by the name of Stephen Alexander. He was a tight end from a place called Chickasha, Oklahoma. It couldn't have been too remote, because he was one of the top-rated recruits in the entire country. He wound up signing with his home state Sooners, becoming an All-American and having a long career in the NFL. On this Sunday though, all our minds were on our stomachs, not the NFL. The amount of food we put away was worthy of a reality TV show. A wild guess is that the bill ran close to $2,000.

After dinner, I was introduced to my host, Coach Erickson's oldest son, Bryce. He was a freshman quarterback for the Canes who was redshirting that first season. Bryce and I really hit it off, and we remain friends to this day. He was the classic son of a coach. He was personable, because he had to make new friends every time his dad took a new job, and he was a real student of the game. He also had good roots – his mom, Marilyn, grew up in Great Falls. Bryce was a great host and this trip was nothing less than epic. After dinner, we dropped our stuff at the hotel and then headed over to grab two fun-loving Canes defensive tackles for a night on the town. Warren Sapp was only a sophomore then, still two years away from being a first-round draft pick, while Dwayne Johnson was a seasoned veteran, having started on the 1991 title team, but still years away from achieving true fame as the movie star, "The Rock." It's amazing to reflect on the similarities between myself and these future stars even when we were just starting out. We all had the same drive, the same focus, and yes sometimes the unbridled confidence that can be considered an attitude problem, but in the end we all want the same thing, to be the best and to win.

We stopped by a music store – I remember this vividly because it was such a metaphor for how out of my world I was – and I bought Snoop Doggy Dog's first solo album, called Doggystyle. My thinking was sound: The CD probably wouldn't be in Great Falls for another month, and my mother wouldn't let me buy it there anyway. We bumped that CD all over town that night. I remember feeling so free and uninhibited in this new and unfamiliar place. We headed to Dan Marino's Bar and Grill for the evening and this was truly my first experience of how football players are treated differently. I don't know if this was just Miami or the way it is all over the country, but we were waved in like royalty. I was 17 years old and there was no check of my ID or anyone else's. The bouncer just gave a fist jab to Bryce and away we went.

This was like watching a movie, only I was in the middle of it. People would just come over and introduce themselves and buy us drinks and food. People were telling me how great I was and how I needed to be a Cane. What? Really? You know who I am? You've heard of Great Falls?

Bryce started introducing me to one beautiful and exotic looking woman after another. I'm not sure if it was the flannel shirt or my immaturity, but none of them seemed particularly wowed by me. When it came to hitting on the ladies, I had no game whatsoever. For me, it was the worst of all worlds – I'd either get really shy or very pretentious.

The night was a whirlwind and lasted into the early hours of the morning. I had my very first experience with alcohol, Bacardi

Rum, and I was pretty anxious about it, but after the first one I had a second, then a third. I was off like a race horse. 'When In Rome' I guess. I didn't anticipate coming back here so I figured what the hell, compromise your principles, just follow the crowd and be free. As we left the bar there was a limo waiting outside to take us away. Bryce was adamant that there would be no driving after drinking, so he magically summoned the limo. Before heading back to the hotel, we stopped to pick up a couple more Canes ballplayers and kept on drinking. In the midst of all the excitement, I somehow decided to announce to everyone that I was going to become a Cane. Cheers rang throughout the limo. And then I thought to myself, "What the hell did you just say?"

Christ, I was like a cheap imitation of Arthur, spouting off at the mouth about stuff I had no intention of doing. Unbeknownst to me, Johnson and a couple others decided to initiate me into their Cane gang when we got back to the hotel. They shaved lines into one of my eyebrows. I didn't have the heart to tell them I was just being a blowhard. Plus, it felt great to be with a group of guys who were welcoming me into their club with open arms. The feeling was just like the one I had as a junior at C.M. Russell the year before when all the seniors, who I so wanted to impress, embraced me as one of their own. I didn't feel that way with the guys in my own class during the just-concluded season and it was a void for me. While the warm welcome was great, the result – lines shaved into my right eyebrow – made me look like a goofball. At least no tattoos were involved.

I was so tired the next day during all the academic meetings, I grabbed one of the graduate assistants and asked if I could find a place to take a quick nap. I explained that I had a basketball game against the cross town rivals the following night and really needed to rest. He just looked at me and laughed and then walked me to his office and said I could crash on the couch for a few hours. I said thanks and we then introduced ourselves. His name was Eric Price.

Talk about irony. Here I was being recruited at one end of the country by Mike Price at Washington State and at the other end by a Miami Hurricanes staff that included Mike's oldest son. It's a small world sometimes, but football really makes it that way. Mike and Dennis were old friends who grew up together in Everett and now Eric was getting his coaching start at what arguably was the best program in the nation at the time. Years later, after Eric and I had become friends, he told me how he had been calling his dad throughout my Miami visit to tell him how much I was enjoying it. Eric had heard through the grapevine that I had declared my plans to become a Cane so he may have had a little extra incentive to keep calling his dad.

The real highlight of the trip wasn't the partying. It was my sit-down interview with Coach Erickson after my nap. I walked into his office and quickly felt at home because the décor had a Northwest feel about it. The first thing he said was how nice it was to have a Montana kid looking at the program. He then took me by surprise when he said they'd like to turn me into a tight end. I was stunned, actually. I was a quarterback, I had always been a quarterback, and I always would be a quarterback. While I was taken aback by the idea, I must say I really respected his honesty. Some coaches will tell a kid anything. Coach Erickson was totally up-front with me.

He then again caught me off guard when he brought up all the speculation going on about him possibly moving on to the NFL.

He was very up front with me. He wasn't going to jump at any job, but if there ever was an opening with the Seattle Seahawks he'd take a hard look at it. His honesty blew me away. National titles aside, my view of him as a coach and person skyrocketed. The idea of playing for Miami, as a tight end, under someone other than Dennis Erickson, made about as much sense as wearing a flannel shirt in southern Florida.

My mom had been against this trip all along. As I boarded the plane for home, her words of concern were playing in my head. The big city, the glamorous program, and my impulsive personality seemed like a recipe for trouble. It was actually Coach Lubick from Colorado State who assured her that this trip would be okay. A few nights before I departed, he told her to let me go, let me enjoy myself and take it all in. "I guarantee it, he will not go to Miami," he told her. They were both right in a way, I did get impulsive and caught up in the hype but I knew that I would never truly be happy there. I'm a Montana boy, a mountain and stream kid. I landed back in Great Falls in time to catch my last few classes of the day. In basketball we were playing Great Falls High, our arch-rival, that night. Their coaches tried to get me ruled ineligible for the game because I hadn't attended all my classes that day. Right there in the span of about ten hours I had seen the best and worst of what athletics has to offer – Dennis Erickson, coach of the "renegade" Miami Hurricanes, being completely forthright with me about the future, and a high school coach resorting to petty nonsense to give his team an advantage.

It was a big day for me. In the morning, Coach Erickson had helped move me closer to a college decision. In the evening, I hit two free throws with two seconds left to seal our victory over the Bison and set off an impromptu celebration that spilled onto the court and eventually into the street. It was an interesting ride I was on, and it was only going to get more interesting.

Six weeks later, on letter of intent signing day, I learned why Coach Erickson envisioned me playing tight end. He signed two – yes, two – quarterbacks who were each rated among the top six high school QB prospects in the country, Scott Covington of Laguna Niguel, Calif., and Ryan Clement of Denver. The Canes' cupboard at quarterback was now so full that Bryce Erickson decided to transfer to a junior college. It's funny how things work out, how one decision on one day – by you or someone else – can completely alter the path you're on.

My path was pointing toward Pullman, but there were still some exit signs, to Boulder, Fort Collins and Eugene, that I had to resist before fully committing.

THE CALL THAT CHANGED IT ALL

Somewhere amid a flurry of J.J. Stokes receptions and an avalanche of Brent Moss rushing yards, the telephone rang. My mom, in the kitchen, called to me in the living room, "Ryan, phone!" Right in the middle of the Rose Bowl. I thought, 'Who would call somebody in the middle of the Rose Bowl?'

Clearly not a sports fan, I reasoned. It was New Year's Day of 1994 and the Wisconsin Badgers were going to win their first Granddaddy ever. As I walked over to grab the phone, I kept my eye on the television. I didn't want to miss a play. Football was not a sport, it was an obsession. When I said hello, the voice on the other end boomed back, "Hey Ryan, Coach Price."

"Hi Coach," I said, probably sounding a little surprised that it was him. He asked how I was and what I was doing. I told him I was watching the Rose Bowl. We talked a bit about the ball game and how things had been going for me. Then he said something I didn't expect. "Ryan, I'll make you a deal. If you come to Washington State, you and I will play in that game together!"

45

Just like that, in the blink of an eye, my mind transported me from the family living room in Great Falls to the middle of the Rose Bowl in Pasadena. It was probably a very simple, even gratuitous, thing to say and any coach could have said that to me. But no one else did. Mike Price did. And I bought in hook, line and sinker. I said, "Hell yes, coach – I would love that." Ryan Leaf in the Rose Bowl. That sounded good, real good.

Of course, I had no idea at the time, and wouldn't realize it for a couple more years, but Washington State hadn't actually been to the Rose Bowl since 1931. I believed in Mike, and I know for a fact he believed in his heart that Pasadena was our destiny.

I was now sold. I got off the phone and walked into my parents' bedroom and announced that I was going to Wazzu. I was going to be a Cougar. They both looked at me in bewilderment, because up to this point I was really keeping my options open, and had an official visit to Oregon coming up soon. They knew how I sometimes jumped the gun on things, but on this one I think they could see the conviction in my eyes. Mike Price said we're going to the Rose Bowl together. End of discussion. "Well, okay," they said, and I walked back to the living room to finish watching the Bruins and Badgers.

My folks would later tell me they were relieved I had made this decision, on my own and with my gut. They quietly rejoiced, probably not wanting to be too vocal for fear I might change my mind before signing day. They trusted Coach Price and liked everyone they'd met from the school. They also liked the family feel of Pullman.

I sat there watching the rest of the Rose Bowl game and started to daydream about playing on that lush, green grass in front of 100,000 rabid fans, and seeing the words "Washington State" painted in one of the end zones. It was now there, planted in my subconscious, as the ultimate goal.

I spent the better part of the next few days calling other coaches to let them know I was going to WSU and that my decision was firm. This wasn't an easy process. Breaking the news to Coach Lubick at Colorado State broke my heart because he had been so kind to me and my parents. He was disappointed but respectful of my decision and said he wished me nothing but success. In his heart, I think he knew there was no way he could say anything to stop me from going to a conference like the Pac-10. My conversation with Brian Cabral was especially painful. He was the assistant coach at Colorado in charge of recruiting me and had probably sent at least twice the number of cards and letters to me as any other school. As far back as I could remember, I wanted to be a Colorado Buffalo, and he was Mr. Buffalo. A Buffs linebacker in the 1970s, he returned as a coach after playing in the NFL. He remains there, coaching linebackers, to this very day. I had developed a great relationship with him and really valued our friendship. Developing tight bonds like that had always been hard for me, but when I did I was as loyal as the day is long. My voice probably cracked when I called him. He was amazingly gracious and understanding. But he wasn't going to give up just yet, asking me to take a couple days to think it over. When I told him I was crimson through and through, he knew I wasn't budging. The Buffs were already in pretty good hands at quarterback, with Koy Detmer and Kordell Stewart, so I'm not sure losing me was that big a deal but he sure made me feel loved.

I called UCLA, Miami and Wyoming to let them know. Wyoming had been a bit of a dark horse in recruiting me, but I hadn't officially crossed them off the list until now. The head coach was Joe Tiller, another old Montana State ballplayer, as well as a one-time WSU assistant coach, who impressed me. He was a firm believer in the spread offense, which of course attracted me, and the Cowboys had just concluded a great year, going 8-4 and appearing in the Copper Bowl.

Finally there was just one more call to make, to Mike Bellotti, the offensive coordinator at Oregon. I put this one off to the end because I had a recruiting trip with them scheduled for just a few days away. I had a sinking feeling I might get scolded, so I tried to put the call off as long as possible. My instinct was right. Man, was Bellotti upset. The anger boiled over out of every word he spoke. He told me this was a poor decision and that I should at least visit Eugene and see what they had to offer. He told me the Cougars would never reach the Rose Bowl and that we'd never beat the Ducks. I was stunned at his bad-mouthing of the Cougs and became bitter about it. Years later, in thinking back on it, I came to a very different conclusion. He was angry because he really wanted me to play for him, and he'd invested a lot of time and effort in trying to make that happen. For the record, my bitterness didn't subside until after I left Pullman. We beat the Ducks three times in the four years I was there. In the two games I started against them we scored a collective 79 points. I was motivated just a bit.

Another difficulty that arose from my decision to go to WSU stemmed from my coach and mentor at C.M. Russell High, Jack Johnson. Coach Johnson had been someone I'd looked up to for as long as I could remember. He was, and is, widely respected in the coaching ranks throughout the Rocky Mountain region. I believe he was disappointed I didn't really include him in my decision-making process. He also was friends with Coach Lubick at Colorado State and knew I'd be in good, trusted hands if I went there. I think Wyoming might have been one of his preferences as well. Now I was going to Pullman. He didn't believe this was the right decision and let me know about it darn near every chance he had. I never understood that thinking. Going to a Pac-10 school, with a head coach like Mike Price, seemed like a pretty nice score to me. The depth of Coach Johnson's ire was even deeper than I thought. When a magazine came out profiling all of WSU's new recruits for 1994, the quotes about me from him only pointed out my shortcomings. Everyone else in the class had nothing but glowing things said about them. It was so out-of-place that Coach Price was later asked if he'd somehow recruited a dud at quarterback.

But that's the nature of the beast. Sports is an emotion-filled roller coaster ride. The time, energy and effort that goes into it is huge and the payoff is that you get to test yourself in front of a bunch of people who are either yelling for you at the top of their lungs or against you at the top of their lungs. This is a pursuit that is filled with emotion and subjectivity. When things don't break your way or the way you think they ought to, you need to vent. That's what Mike Bellotti had done when I called him. And it's what Coach Johnson did when I told him my plans. I was confused, sad and angry when it happened – he no longer called me "The Leafster," which I always loved – but the passage of time has given me greater perspective on the forces that shape how and why people, including me, react the way they do in certain situations.

After finishing all of those difficult phone calls and conversations, I was at peace with my decision and knew that it was the right one. I had done it, I had decided to accept an athletic scholarship to play football at Washington State University. I was going to be a Cougar. I had no real idea what kind of commitment that I was making at the time – a commitment to an identity that would define me for the rest of my life.

Signing day, on February 2nd, was no big deal like it tends to be today with kids having ceremonies. I got up early, like I did most days, to practice shooting free throws, and then came in and signed my letter of intent on the kitchen table. I handed it to my dad, who took it to work and faxed it to the football office at WSU. Symbolically, it couldn't have been more poetic – my loving dad of 17 years handing me off to a stand-in dad who would take me under his wing and guide me for the next four years. At both ends of that fax, I think two tremendous men we're uttering "Go Cougs!" at about the same time.

RIDIN' WITH THE POSSE

"God dammit, Leaf. Throw the ball where I tell you to throw it."

Craig Bray was angry. He had seen enough, and came running in from the secondary just to make extra sure I could hear him hollering at me. The guy normally looked about as mild-mannered as the standard dad in a TV sit-com, but whoa Nellie could he get fired up.

We were both rookies in 1994, though he had just a bit more experience than me and a whole lot more say in how practices were conducted. So when I went off script as the scout team quarterback, he went ballistic in his role as the assistant coach in charge of the defensive backs.

Coach Bray was actually in his second stint at WSU. He had been there in 1987-88 before moving on to Miami with Dennis Erickson. He had just returned to WSU after several years as the defensive coordinator at Idaho. He would stay in Pullman through the 1999 season, and help develop some of the greatest defensive

51

backs in school history. In 1994 he might have thought he'd been set up mostly to pop a vein, because he was spending a lot of time vocalizing my direction. Maybe not on a daily basis, but often enough that I'm sure both of us could cite the routine in our sleep. Here's how it went. Mike Walker, a one-time co-captain of the Cougs who was just starting his coaching career and overseeing the scout team, would hold up cards of what play he wanted us to run and what receiver the ball should go to. To liven things up a bit, I'd drop back to pass and go through my regular progressions until I found an open receiver and fired. I didn't want to just throw the ball into coverage. It's not natural for a quarterback – even the scout team quarterback – to want to do that.

Coach Bray would come unglued when I did this. His outbursts could make the drill sergeant from *Full Metal Jacket* look like a pansy. Don't get me wrong, Coach Bray was, and is, a very good man and excellent coach. It's just that he could really light up like a Roman candle. His ire at me also roped in Coach Walker, because he was supposed to be in charge of me. I always had the sense defensive coordinator Bill Doba and outside linebackers coach Jim Zeches thought this was more amusing, and even refreshing, than disruptive. They were two of the most even-keeled guys around.

All in all, it's a good thing Coach Bray was the secondary coach, because if he had been the head man I would have been so far into the doghouse I'd have never been let out. "What are you trying to do – make me develop poor habits?" I'd retort when he'd yell at me for not throwing the ball where he wanted it.

"This is not about you, Leaf," he'd say back, at a decibel level that might have been heard all the way over to Greek Row. "This is about the defense getting better and getting ready to play on Saturday."

The great thing about the scout team is that redshirts and deep backups get a chance to play every day. The bad thing about the scout team is that you're only mimicking that week's opponents for the benefit of the starters. So throwing balls into coverage is expected from the quarterback. Whenever you read a practice report that says so-and-so on defense intercepted a pass, it's most likely a bunch of BS if the guy's a first stringer because odds are the scout team QB was forced to throw the ball in there.

My freelancing efforts didn't end with the play calling. I made a little game where I would pick one defensive player each week and try to get under his skin. It probably wasn't the wisest move on my part because as the scout team QB I was going up against the first-string defense – and this was no ordinary defense. This was the Palouse Posse. Fast, ferocious and smart. These guys were as a good a college defense as you'll ever see. I think all 11 starters went on to play in the NFL or CFL. As the defensive coordinator, Bill Doba loved to attack, and with the speed the Posse possessed he was in full assault mode.

One of the big stars was future Seattle Seahawk Chad Eaton of Puyallup. He was a senior defensive tackle, big and mean, and cocky as can be. One day we got up to the line of scrimmage and I barked out, "Down, set, Eaton sucks, Eaton sucks . . . " Naturally, Eaton and his mates weren't very impressed, so I kept doing it. They became downright angry and started coming after me and going out of their way to knock me down. I kept getting back up and doing it again. Every week. "Down, set, Mark Fields is a pussy,

Mark Fields is a pussy . . . John Rushing is about to get his ass burned, John Rushing is about to get his ass burned . . ." I'm sure they thought I was a crackpot, especially when I didn't stop. I took a pretty good beating. The whole season went on like that, back and forth, with those guys pitching me as much verbal abuse as physical. Along with Eaton, senior defensive back Torey Hunter of Tacoma, and junior linebacker Chris Hayes of California, were easily as good at trash talking as I was.

Verbal jousting aside, these guys were a huge part of my development as a quarterback because they were so good. I had to bring my best to the field every day just to keep my head above water. I think they probably accelerated my development by two years. This tells you how good the Posse was: Greg Burns, a standout defensive back from '93, missed all of '94 with an injury and his replacement was Brian Walker – a guy who would later play eight years in the NFL. The Posse finished the '94 season rated the No. 2 defense in the nation. As a team, we had an 8-4 record and beat Baylor 10-3 in the Alamo Bowl. Unfortunately, our offense struggled horribly all season, otherwise this could have been a team competing for the national title. We averaged only 16 points per game – and it seemed like the defense set up most of those points. In six games we scored 10 points or less.

One of the great highlights of my WSU career came that season in our last practice before the Apple Cup. As practice ended, the Posse circled around and then hoisted me on their shoulders and carried me off the field. These were some of the finest players ever to wear crimson – Ron Childs, Singor Mobley, DeWayne Patterson, Don Sasa, Dwayne Sanders, et. al. Talk about validating. I had earned the respect of a group of truly great players. I had competed with them hard for 12 straight weeks and through fall camp and this was their way of saying thanks. Even in high school, I thirsted for the respect of the upper classmen. So to get it in my first year at WSU was beyond gratifying and really helped lay a foundation for the future.

The seniors on the Posse were three years removed from our great 1997 team that went to the Rose Bowl. But from my perspective, they were instrumental in helping get us to Pasadena.

FROM TRAGEDY COMES UNITY

"You know, I'm going to be a great college quarterback. I'm big, I've got a great arm and I love to win. You should have seen some of my games this season. I was torching defenses. There were DBs and linebackers who looked like deer in the headlights."

Those words, or something very close to them, were uttered by Yours Truly one December evening in 1993 at the Holiday Inn Express in Pullman. I was a high school senior on my official recruiting trip to WSU and I was talking with Jason McEndoo, a Cougar offensive lineman from the tiny logging town of Cosmopolis on the Washington coast. He was a redshirting freshman at the time and one of my hosts for the weekend.

Either I was too dim to realize it or Jason was a great actor, but I had no idea at the time that he was thinking I was the biggest piece of work he'd ever come across. Hearing him tell the story years later, how I was going on and on about how great I was, and how great I was going to be was humbling, embarrassing and hilarious all at the same time.

Here was a guy who was many things I wasn't. He was mature beyond his years, for instance. And while he was a heck of a football player and true student of the game, he was also a talented artist. He loved to draw and paint, and once won a national cartoon drawing contest. For me, playing ball and dreaming about females was about all I had time for outside of school.

The thought of me serving as the leader of a team Jason McEndoo was on seems, in retrospect, farfetched. But things have a way of working out.

Sometimes.

Other times, things go very, very wrong. Even horribly, tragically wrong.

Fast forward from that recruiting trip in 1993 to the summer of 1996. In June, Jason married Michelle Wild, his Aberdeen High sweetheart and fellow WSU student. There must have been invisible cupids in the air because a month later all of us were in Tacoma for fellow teammate Cory Withrow's wedding. Michelle sang. Jason and his best friend and fellow Cougar lineman, Ryan McShane, were groomsmen. It was an amazing celebration.

The next day, life as we knew it would change forever. Jason, Michelle, and Ryan were driving back to Pullman from the wedding. The McEndoos' truck was on the fritz so they had carpooled with Ryan, who had originally been planning to fly. About two miles outside of Ellensburg, Ryan nodded off briefly and his Ford Explorer swerved. He woke up and overcorrected, and the Explorer flipped several times. Jason came out of the accident mostly unhurt and Ryan was bruised and battered after being ejected through the sun roof. Michelle was sleeping in the back seat and thrown out of the back window. She died at the scene. She was 22 and had been married to Jason for 29 days.

I remember getting back to Pullman and hearing the message on my answering machine about what happened. I couldn't believe what I was hearing. I spent the next few weeks trying to find a way to put things in perspective. How do we deal with this as a team? How do I comfort Jason and Ryan as well? Will the season be lost, because all of us now realize so starkly that football doesn't mean as much as it did before?

There were so many issues to deal with. For the next few weeks, teammates and I would visit Jason at the doublewide trailer he and Michelle had outside of Pullman. None of us knew what to say or what to really do in this situation. And it wasn't just Jason who was hurting, either. Ryan, as the driver, was devastated. The "what ifs," he would say, just ate at him. It was probably a year before he'd even get behind the wheel of a car.

We all tried to come together for Jason and Ryan that fall camp and attempt to put the pieces back together. As we prepared for the first game, at Colorado, Jason came to the offensive linemen and me and asked us to wear an "M" on our jersey in remembrance of Michelle. I was so honored that he would ask me to do that. I wore that jersey with so much pride I don't think he truly understands how much it meant.

We lost badly to Colorado in that first game and it was clear Jason's focus wasn't on the field. I don't remember the exact details, but our team's sports psychologist, Jim Bauman, later called all the offensive linemen together to talk about Michelle's death and how best to help Jason. Jim had been talking with Jason regularly since the accident but there had never been a group meeting of the linemen like this. I wasn't there, but I understand it was very emotional for everyone and helped get the friendship between Jason and Ryan back on track.

The next week we had to travel all the way to Philadelphia to play the Temple Owls. It was a back-and-forth battle until the last minute. With beautiful protection from the entire offensive line, I hit Chad Carpenter for the game-winning touchdown in the corner of the end zone. We came to the sideline and everyone was going crazy, jumping up and down in celebration. I looked down the bench and saw Jason alone, his head in his hands, and then Ryan coming over and sitting next to him. I walked down and saw that they both were crying uncontrollably and I knelt down between them both and witnessed the raw emotion of being part of a family, being there for one another in the face of everything and being able to lean on your fellow Cougar when he needed it the most. While everyone around us was in joyous celebration we hugged one another and let our true emotions explode. I remember that game vividly. Jason let us in and made us a part of his family and allowed us to help. Being a teammate and a Cougar had allowed him to heal a little bit on that hot, humid night, and brought all of us closer than we could have imagined.

Jason, who would later play a couple of seasons in the NFL, is now a well-respected college coach. He is remarried to another fellow Cougar, Ruth Padgett, who entered his life when he truly needed her. They have four kids and have built a wonderful family and life together. They continue to be an inspiration to me. I believe in my heart that through the tragedy Jason endured in 1996 he embraced what took me such a long time to figure out – that letting people into your heart and mind is the only path to true healing. When I think of Jason, I see a tremendously courageous and heroic human being.

MY MELTING POT

There are two stereotypes in sports that drive me nuts. The first is an old one: Jocks are dumb. I think the ongoing promotion of all-academic selections and team GPAs is helping reduce that old kind of thinking, but the stereotype is so off base it's ridiculous. I know that playing quarterback in college and the pros has to be about as mentally demanding a job as there is outside of medicine, warfare and space exploration. For proof, I look at my GPA at WSU. During football season, my grades were horrible, maybe around 2.0 if I'm being optimistic, largely because all my time and energy was directed at playing ball. Outside the season, my grades were all As and Bs. So next time you hear someone speak the phrase "dumb jock," do me a favor and tell them to think twice. We're working full time, representing the university in a very physically and mentally demanding pursuit, and also staying on track to earn a college degree. There's nothing dumb about that. It takes drive, discipline and determination.

61

The second stereotype that just kills me is about black athletes, and I hear it darn near every time I turn on the TV. If a black player is good, the media and some fans say, it's because of his natural athleticism. By contrast, standout white players are portrayed as good because they work hard and have high IQs. Pay close attention to football or basketball broadcasts around the country this season and I guarantee you'll hear that star white players are scrappy, while star black players "make it look easy." That's the kind of subtle racism that still exists in America and it's time it ended. Anyone playing college sports was born with natural athleticism and anyone who succeeds at it must work hard. The color of your skin has nothing to do with it.

Black athletes are also often stereotyped as coming from single-parent homes and drug-infested, bullet-riddled neighborhoods. There are guys with those tough backgrounds, no question, and their stories – of one which I'll share in a moment – are inspirational. But I think the media are so focused on those stories that they've created this impression around the country that there are no black kids who come from standard, boring middle- and upper-middle class families. That's pretty much what I thought coming out of high school.

So imagine my surprise when Kearney Adams, a 5-foot-9, 160-pound receiver from Gilbert, Arizona, approached me one day my freshman year to talk about golf. Golf? What? You're black!

I know, talk about naïve, clueless and unworldly. That was me.

Kearney was a JC transfer on the team who also happened to be African-American and an avid golfer. He's one of the most personable, likeable people on the face of the earth. He had heard

I liked golf and soon we became friends. He was older than I was, and really took on something of a big brother role with me. I used to jokingly tell people that Kearney was my first black friend. But it was no joke. I grew up in Great Falls. There's not a lot of diversity in north-central Montana. I think we had one black person in my high school. When I arrived at WSU, I saw all these black ballplayers and immediately presumed they were all bad asses from the 'hood. Now here comes Kearney Adams breaking all those stereotypes I'd seen on TV.

Being a quarterback and receiver, Kearney and I naturally spent a lot of time together on the field, but whenever there might be a window of down time we'd try to head over to the golf course to hit balls or maybe play nine. We were fierce competitors but it never got in the way of our friendship. Kearney's girlfriend – and now wife – was Jenni Ruff. That name might sound familiar because she was on the Cougar basketball team and wound up being probably the greatest women's player in WSU history. I was always trying to get her to fix me up with somebody else on the basketball team so I could be like Kearney – a football player with a beautiful basketball player on my arm. That never worked out, but facts were facts with Kearney: He was my first confidant, my first real friend, somebody I could always come to with stuff. He was very intelligent, very mature, and very capable – a true mentor and leader. That was important for me that freshman season because I was socially awkward and not making friends easily. Kearney took the initiative to extend a hand to me and I'm eternally grateful he did. We remain friends to this day. Every year I go visit him and Jenn and their three beautiful kids in Arizona.

It was only appropriate that Kearney was on the receiving end of my first big completion as a college player. In 1995, my second year in the program and his last, we played the University of Montana in our home opener. I played the last half of the fourth quarter, and checked into a play called 96X, which meant Kearney would run a corner out from the inside. I threw a deep ball and Kearney made a tremendous move to get to it. He hauled it in and was tackled just inside the 10-yard line. That was my first notable completion.

Kearney and I loved being on the field at the same time because we knew what the other guy was thinking in almost any situation. Later that 1995 season, when I made my first start – in the Apple Cup – we were able to cap off our friendship with a touchdown pass. It would be our one and only, because Kearney was a senior. It happened in the second half of a tight game. We ran a post wheel route. I ran a counter boot fake, then set up in the pocket, and stepped into a throw. Kearney was all alone down the sideline and made an unbelievable catch over his outside shoulder. Somehow, some way, he tip-toed his way into the end zone for a TD. He did a little celebration dance and the smile on my face was a mile wide. My only regret, outside the fact we lost the game on a last-minute field goal, was that he wouldn't be around for my final two seasons at WSU.

While Kearney was "my first black friend," he was far from the only one. Kevin McKenzie, one of our Fab Five receivers, was in fact the guy from south-central Los Angeles who had a serious hill to climb to earn his college degree. About the only thing different from Kevin's story than the stereotypical one you tend to see on TV or read about is that while his parents were never married, both were very present, very involved in his life. Kevin grew up in south-central L.A. in a building made out of concrete cinder blocks. A few days before the 1998 Rose Bowl, Dick Rockne, a long-time Seattle Times sports writer, went with him back to the old neighborhood and the memories came flooding back. Drug dealers in fancy cars and gang members looking to take your new tennis shoes were as normal to Kevin as trout fishing and deer hunting were to me. He talked about the Fourth of July when he was seven years old, when a different kind of popping noise erupted outside and then a family friend came stumbling into the McKenzie apartment covered in blood and holding his side. That's a lot to overcome for a kid. What Cougar fans remember most about Kevin was "The Catch" to beat USC. What I remember most was a thoughtful, hard-working young man who overcame a lot and graduated from college.

In retrospect, I cringe at this thought, but I must admit that in 1994 when I arrived in Pullman my sheltered existence in Montana had me wondering if I'd be able to connect with guys from the inner city. Some spoke differently than I did. Some listened to what I thought was strange music. Some dressed differently. Some were very guarded, not sure who could and couldn't be trusted. I was really unsure of myself. When people think of sports teams, I don't get the sense they view us as anything but a bunch of athletes. But we're really a melting pot of personalities, cultures and backgrounds. It's really quite a great thing when we're thrown together, because it forces you out of your comfort zone and makes you look at the world from new perspectives.

The day before that Montana game in '95, it really struck me how WSU was this giant melting pot. My parents were in town and

Chris Hayes, our senior co-captain and stud linebacker, came up to me and my dad and asked if we knew Dave Dickenson, Montana's star quarterback. "He grew up just a block down the street from us," my dad explained. Chris then says, "If you see him, tell him I'm going for his ass. I'm going to beat his ass into the ground." In Great Falls, nobody ever talked like that, and certainly not to a teammate's 45-year-old dad whom he'd never met before. My dad just looked on politely. Where Chris grew up, in San Bernardino east of Los Angeles, that was the way it was.

So we were thrown together in Pullman, black and white, big-city kids and small-town kids, all surrounded by a sea of wheat. It's a great eye-opener about diversity. Chris grew up in a county – a single county – with twice as many people in it as there are in all of Montana. We didn't just come from different places, we damn near came from different planets. Chris even had some of his teeth capped in gold, just in case anyone wasn't sure how badass he was. Everyone called him Pedo. I have no idea why, but my guess is that it was short for torpedo. And that would fit – fast and explosive. We got along great, and my earlier worries that I wouldn't know how to interact with the black guys from California vanished – so much so that I subconsciously started adopting some of their slang and inflections as my own.

Chris was as tough as they come. He had spent some time in a correctional facility in his early high school days and said if it weren't for one of the counselors there as well as his high school coach, he's not sure what path he may have gone down in life. And now here he was the co-captain of a Pac-10 football team and on the verge of what would become a long career (complete with a Super

66

Bowl ring) in the NFL. The old phrase that it takes a village to raise a child really held true with Chris. It's probably no surprise that he had tremendous heart and character. He cared about every game, every snap, every tick of the clock. So much so, that I understand he now runs his own company and does motivational speaking on the side.

I was a first-hand beneficiary of Chris' leadership skills and character at the end of that 1995 season. In our third-to-last game, at Cal, Coach Price sent me out onto the field in the second quarter and basically alternated Chad Davis and me the rest of the game. I was as nervous as a cat in a dog house. This wasn't mop up time and it wasn't Montana. This was a Pac-10 game. After my first series, Chris knew I was unsettled and he came up to me on the sidelines and was very encouraging, really bolstering my confidence. I'm not sure how it transpired, because I was back on the field when it happened, but at some point during the game Davis confronted Chris about being so supportive to me. The two of them got into an argument right there on the sidelines. That was pretty much the end for Chad. He didn't take a snap the final two games of the season and eventually transferred to a Division I-AA school. For Chris, it was just another case of being a good leader and stand-up guy. Those are the types of individuals – regardless of race, color or religion – you want to go into battle with on Saturdays because you know your back is covered.

LAYING THE FOUNDATION

The roots of any successful pursuit can be traced to countless people, decisions and twists of fate, and our 1997 season was no different. Milestones that led to who and what we would become could be tracked to the schoolings the Palouse Posse gave the scout team in 1994, the junior varsity game we played against Walla Walla Community College in 1995, and so many other experiences along the way. The biggest building block of all was the 1996 season, which started out with great promise and ended as a tale of lessons learned and opportunities squandered.

The sportswriters picked us to finish ninth in the Pac-10 in 1996, but people in and around the program knew we had the talent to get to the post season. The WSU media guide made no secret of those expectations, explaining that, "The return of a salty, veteran loaded defense and six starters on offense brings a knowing smile to head coach Mike Price's face as the 1996 football season draws near ... (he) believes the combination of 14 returning starters and a defense that could rival the 1993 and 1994 squads will produce an outstanding season with a third bowl bid in his tenure a distinct possibility."

The defense included honors candidates like James Darling, Johnny Nansen and Dorian Boose, while the offense featured the likes of veterans David Knuff, Chad Carpenter, Jason McEndoo and soon-to-be All-American Scott Sanderson. This was also to be the year one Ryan Leaf was supposed to deliver on the high hopes fueled by the 54 points our previously sluggish offense put on the board in the final two games of 1995.

Unlike the previous summer, when much of my "preparation" for the coming season consisted of fishing, golfing and basketball, I'd spent the run up to 1996 lifting weights, running and throwing with Chad Carpenter. Our first game was on the road at fifth-ranked Colorado and I had the good sense to pull a page from the Joe Namath handbook. "We're going to shock the world," I told reporters. That prediction came back to bite me. Colorado stuffed us, 37-19, on national TV. One positive to come from the game was the way I kept fighting until the clock hit zero. I think it endeared me a bit to some of my teammates. While we went home humbled, bloodied, and battered, we were still optimistic, and rattled off three wins in a row over Temple, No. 25 Oregon, and San Jose State. We averaged 48 points in those games and I threw a collective 12 TD passes. This was shaping up to be the season I expected.

In what would become a recurring theme, we played tough in the desert against Arizona and its flex defense the following week, but couldn't close the deal at the end and lost 34-26. We then trounced Oregon State on the road and took down No. 19

California in Pullman, 21-18. I remember a light snow started to come down at kickoff of the Cal game and Pat Barnes, their outstanding quarterback, had a heck of time getting a grip on the football. With the win, we were 5-2 and one game away from being bowl eligible.

What happened over the subsequent four weeks ultimately would be a true building block, I believe, for the success of 1997. We lost four games in a row, two of them in painful nail-biters. You talk about testing character and perseverance, those four weeks did it in multiples. USC was first up on that list. Coach Price had never defeated the Trojans and I had never faced them. We were on a roll and had them coming to Pullman for a TV game. The buzz was in the air. We played a tremendous game but couldn't put the boot on the back of their necks and lost 29-24. I was devastated, having fumbled the ball away in the red zone on what should have been the winning drive. I fell into a funk that lasted for the next 10-plus quarters of football.

We hit the road for games at UCLA and Stanford and just fell on our faces. Lackluster is probably the best word for what happened. In fact, we looked so mediocre that Paul Sorensen, Bob Robertson's color analyst on Cougar radio broadcasts, really took the wood to us. Every missed assignment, bad decision, arm tackle and penalty added up in his eyes to a lack of passion and smarts. "Where's the urgency? Where's your head?" he would ask. In a one-on-one post-game interview with Paul he asked me a question I didn't like. I don't recall it being inflammatory, it just hit my thin skin the wrong way. So when the interview was done, I took off the headset and shattered it on the ground – no doubt a glimpse of how I would react in San Diego two years later when things weren't going my way. Paul wasn't even fazed. He was as intense a competitor as I was and he understood my frustration, but there's a distinction between being intense and being an asshole and I clearly didn't know the boundary. Paul never held that blow-up against me. He was a straight shooter who knew the pressures – and personalities – of the game. His criticisms of us during the UCLA and Stanford games, I should note, landed him in hot water with athletic director Rick Dickson, who thought Paul should tone down the critique. The two of them coexisted for another two years before Paul's 13-year run next to Bob Rob came to an end.

Headed into the Apple Cup, we were 5-5 and still in bowl contention. The Huskies were 8-2 and No. 12 in the nation. They were an 11-point favorite, but I was in the midst of a crisis of confidence that had me in a slump – yet another precursor for my time in San Diego and how I coped with losing. The spread probably should have been 30 points. I even told reporters that maybe the Cougars needed a new guy at quarterback if I couldn't come through in this one. To help get me back in a proper frame of mind, Coach Price put together a highlight tape of some of my best plays.

It didn't help. I played the worst football of my Cougar career in the first two-and-a-half quarters of that Apple Cup. We had 16 total yards of offense at halftime and I was a whopping 3-of-12 passing for no net yards. The Huskies led 24-0. In the third quarter, Coach Price called a timeout solely to get in my face. I had just recovered a ball that had slipped out of my hand on a fake screen wheel to Shawn Tims.

"What the Hell's the problem? What's wrong with you?" he yelled when I arrived at the sideline.

Sulking, I gave the standard kid answer: "Nothing."

"Fine. Let's run the same play."

"Why? They're going to know what we're doing."

"God damn it, Ryan, do what I tell you, please."

You have to love the "please" on the end of that sentence. Only Mike Price could tell a guy what a sorry ass he is and still be mildly polite about it.

Sure enough, we ran the same play and it went for about 50 yards, just past midfield. I hit Kevin McKenzie on a corner smash route on the next play and just like that we're on the Husky three-yard-line. We then ran a fake handoff boot and I walked into the end zone. Fans that had left Martin Stadium were now actually coming back from campus to watch this. I can't explain exactly what happened in my head or arm, but from that point forward the Husky defense couldn't stop us. In all, we scored 24 points in 19 minutes and I threw for 200 fourth-quarter yards. The Apple Cup was headed to overtime for the first time ever.

The Dawgs scored a TD on their overtime possession and then we put ourselves in a bad spot and faced a fourth-down-and-23. In a play that Cougar fans ask me about all the time, I arced one to the left corner of the end zone for my favorite receiver, Chad Carpenter. He made a beautiful catch, and then there was a moment of silence. Was he in bounds? He was ruled out and the Huskies had a 31-24 victory. The official's eyesight must have been superhuman because replays showed Chad's foot not more than an inch or two out.

It was no surprise that Chad was my target on that play. That season we connected 47 times, eight of them going for touchdowns. The year before, when I took over at QB at the end of the season, Chad caught more passes in the final two games than he had in the other nine combined. He made a point in the off-season to work out me with. His thinking was sound: if we could do that much damage in two games, imagine how much we could accomplish in a full season with a full off-season of training. That was typical of Chad. He was a team leader with an outstanding work ethic. Mike Levenseller told a story about arriving at Bohler Gym at 6:30 one morning, two-and-a-half hours before two-a-day drills were commencing. It was Chad's freshman season. Not only was Chad already at Bohler when Levy arrived, but he was fully dressed for practice. Our work together in the off-season and subsequent success on Saturdays served as the blueprint for what the not-yet-named Fab Five and I needed to do before the start of the 1997 season.

After the Apple Cup, Coach Price didn't sugar-coat his words. "I am disappointed for the seniors who won't go out with a winning season or a bowl game. I'm disappointed for our assistant coaches and their families and for the fans who are not going someplace warm for Christmas," he said. He talked about how proud he was that we rallied back from the big deficit, but his real focus was on the disappointment. We had underachieved, plain and simple. Yes, the Michelle McEndoo tragedy was emotionally difficult for the entire team. And yes, the holes left by the graduation losses of big-time players like Chris Hayes, Brian Walker, Dwayne Sanders and Jay Dumas weren't easy to fill. But we should have been better than we were. We started out well and then hit a wall. A record of 5-6 wasn't good enough.

The frustration, in all of us, was palpable. The desire for more was clear. This may be rationalizing, but I firmly believe to this day that if we'd made a minor bowl game that season we wouldn't have been nearly as hungry as we were in 1997. The taste left from '96 made us work harder, push harder, want harder. In 1997 we won the close ball games against UCLA, USC, Oregon, Arizona and Washington. That didn't happen by chance. The foundation was put in place in 1996.

ORDINARY vs. EXTRAORDINARY

We knew we were going to be good. No one else seemed to share that opinion, with seventh place about where most forecasters pegged our Washington State Cougars to finish in 1997. Just to be clear, that was seventh place in the Pac-10, not the country. When all was said and done, we had captured the imagination of a region and delivered on a dream that generations of Cougars never thought they'd realize. You can trot out any number of clichés to describe what we accomplished. They're all true. It was a magical season, and we were a team of destiny.

Getting people to believe in us back in July and August of that year was a whole other story. I don't think anyone thought we'd be bad, just mediocre. And with the two first games of the season scheduled against UCLA and USC – teams WSU hadn't beaten in the same year ever – the safe bet was to dismiss us.

Yet all the signs were there to suggest this team could be something special. Foremost, we had 15 starters and 43 lettermen returning from a 5-6 team that was solid, just not consistent. We

75

were all a year older, wiser and stronger. Some excellent players graduated off that 1996 team, including four who would play professionally in James Darling, Scott Sanderson, Chad Carpenter, and Bryan Chiu. But the young talent coming up through the ranks was stellar. Names like Steve Gleason, Lamont Thompson, Rob Meier, Jonathan Nance, Rian Lindell and Love Jefferson were mostly unheard of outside Pullman before the season. By the end, they were like icons.

Another thing that set this team apart was what we did over the summer: We stayed in Pullman! We trained together and played together. Nowadays, such voluntary summer workouts are not only commonplace but expected by every coaching staff in the country. In the 1990s, that wasn't the case. Some guys would stick around Pullman in the summer and take classes but the majority headed home for a couple of months. Not in the summer of '97. We were on the cusp of being really good in 1996 and felt that '97 could be something special if our preparations went above and beyond. As Jimmy Johnson once said, "the difference between ordinary and extraordinary is that little extra." We weren't going to be ordinary. We did that in '96 and it was frustrating as hell.

I don't recall exactly how the ball got rolling for everyone to stay in Pullman for the summer, but I started talking to people about it after I learned that the Palouse Posse had done it prior to the 1994 season. Like us in '96, they had been on the verge of breaking out the season before but couldn't quite get over the hump. In '94 they became one of the best defenses in the nation and the best in the modern history of WSU football.

For a variety of reasons, not everyone on the team stuck around that summer of '97 but the vast majority – 70 percent or more – did. This was a huge commitment, absolutely huge. Playing ball and going to school is already more than full-time work, so the idea of extended time at home, in your own bed with mom's good cooking, is like a magnetic pull. That summer, we all pretty well compressed our home time to two weeks. In exchange, we awoke at 6 a.m., four days a week, so we could be in the weight room or running the stairs by 6:30. At 7:30 we were on the field for passing drills. At 9, we were either headed to class or on the golf course. At the end of each week the offense and defense would come together for "skeleton" drills – basically 7-on-7 games of touch football minus the linemen. We had a ton of fun in these showdowns, but it was serious business. We were working on real plays, real timing, real mechanics. The glory of a season is found on Saturdays in the fall. The foundation for it is found far from the spotlight, lifting weights, running sprints, studying film and throwing passes when the only coach around is the one in your head.

One major piece of our offense in 1996 and 1997 was running back Michael Black. He was one of a handful of guys who didn't stay in Pullman with us over the summer. Given how dedicated he was and how hard he worked, that fact might sound surprising. Michael had a very good "excuse," though, and I admired him for it. His 2-year-old son and girlfriend lived in Los Angeles, where Michael was from. Michael's own father had been in and out of his life, and now Michael wanted to make sure his little man, Caelin, knew he had a father who cared and would be present whenever he could. "In order to raise your son, a father has to be there. The mother can't do it all," he said in an interview before our '97 season opener.

While he wasn't working out with us in Pullman that summer, Michael was still working out. When he arrived back in Pullman for the start of fall camp he looked like he'd been chiseled out of bronze. As it turns out, his summer routine included endless sprints at USC's track and regular visits to a park in El Segundo that featured a giant sand dune. Bottom to top, the dune spanned about 80 yards and sloped at a 45-degree angle. Michael ran up that thing all summer. He was going to be prepared for the UCLA Bruins on August 30. He was going to break 1,000 rushing yards for the season, which he just missed doing in 1996, and he was going to help the Cougars get to the Rose Bowl. He made it clear that he had goals for himself and the team and he was going to reach them.

You could see the determination in his eyes. Michael Black was a man on a mission. Knowing his past helps explain why he had such focus. In his youth he made some bad decisions and ran with the wrong crowd. At 16, he stole a car and was sent to a correctional facility for six months. At 17, he and some buddies put on ski masks and robbed three women at gunpoint. That landed him in a youth prison for close to two years. He was determined to get on a better path, so he earned his high school diploma and worked as a plumber while behind bars.

Michael had only played football briefly at Dorsey High School in Los Angeles because he spent most of those years incarcerated. It was in his first sentence, at a place called Camp Kirkpatrick, that he really learned the game. They had a team of inmates that played against small high schools in the region. When he got out from behind bars the second time, he headed to West Los Angeles College. In two years there he piled up a mountain of yardage and grabbed the attention of college recruiters. Once they learned about his background, though, they backed off.

With the exception of Mike Price. "He was blunt and honest with me, up front all the way. He is a good person," Mike would later tell columnist Jim Moore about the decision to recruit Michael. "I'm betting my paycheck he's going to stay straight. I'm betting my life and reputation on it."

Michael didn't disappoint. He was a great teammate, a great Cougar, who proved that second – even third – chances in life are worth the investment. Mike Price showed once again the power of one. One person who believes and cares can make all the difference in a life.

Michael was soft spoken, but a powerful leader through his actions, putting in tremendous effort and running as hard on every down as any back I've ever been around, college or pro. Another thing I loved about Michael was that he never complained down at the goal-line when a running play was signaled in and I'd audible to a pass. He rushed for nearly 1,200 yards in 1997 and scored 11 touchdowns, but that TD total really would have been closer to 20 (easily a school record) if I hadn't been such a ball hog.

That summer for all of us, wherever we were, was a huge contributor to who we would become that season.

THE PARTY IS JUST BEGINNING
UCLA: 1997 Game 1

Keith Jackson was coming to town. The old Cougar had called a number of WSU games over the years but never one played in Pullman. This was why we were playing the Bruins on August 30 rather than the originally scheduled date in November: to get on ABC-TV. Jim Walden, the colorful Cougar coach of the 1980s, said Mike Price had made either the best decision of his career or the worst in agreeing to move this game. California guys aren't used to the cold of November, he noted. On the other hand, the toll of injuries late in the season gives an edge to the team with the greater depth and that would tend to favor UCLA.

Jim had experience with this kind of schedule tampering. Twelve years earlier to the day, in 1985, he had WSU's great RPM backfield of Mark Rypien, Kerry Porter, and Rueben Mayes squaring off in Pullman against Oregon. Hopes were high that season. The Oregon game had been planned for November but the opportunity for TV prompted the change to August. The game was a doozy, Jim says, but the Cougs lost 42-39 and the team's confidence was shot. They won only four games that season.

There was another twist to us opening up with the Bruins. By doing so, it meant our first two games of the year would be against the Los Angeles schools. Following the Bruins, we would have a bye and then a trip to USC. In short, our season effectively could be over by sunset on September 13. Or maybe, just maybe, we could be in the driver's seat for the Rose Bowl.

Based on the attendance that day in Pullman, I'm guessing not too many folks were thinking we were a team about to launch a historic run. The crowd only numbered 26,000, but I must say they sounded like 50,000. They were in this one pretty much from start to finish, with the Leaf clan out in force. There was always a good family contingent at every home game but for this one – maybe because it was Labor Day weekend – we had relatives from all over Montana in town.

On offense and defense, we had a great week of preparation coming into this game. I felt very confident in our game plan. And then I was thrown a curve. Little things before games aren't supposed to sidetrack you, but being a superstitious guy, I was just stunned when one of the game officials came up to me during warm ups and told me I couldn't wear my socks so high. I loved my high socks, all the way past the knee. These were the same socks I'd worn the entire 1996 season, and now I was being told they're illegal. This was too weird. He said I had to have space between the tops of my socks and bottoms of my pants. I actually sat in the locker room and stewed about it for a little bit, and wondered how my socks had anything to do with anything. I had no choice, so I rolled them down about five inches. Coach Price got some sort of waiver for me for the rest of the season but to this day I scratch my head over "Sock-Gate."

On the opening kickoff, we pinned the Bruins on their own two, and I was salivating at the field position we'd have after they punted. Two snaps later, Skip Hicks ran up the middle for a 92-yard gain, and two plays after that he scored the first of his four touchdowns on the day.

When it was our turn, we drove right down the field, but I could see we still had some of those first-game jitters. Sure enough, on second-and-goal, Kevin McKenzie dropped what would have been a walk-in touchdown on an out-and-in route. That was totally uncharacteristic of Kevin. On the next play I tried a QB draw and just about had my head taken off. I went rolling across the turf like a rag doll, my lip bleeding. The tone for the day was set. This was going to be a back-and-forth brawl. Rian Lindell kicked a field goal for us and it was 7-3.

On our second series on offense, I saw my season flash before my eyes. I rolled my right ankle. This was one of those full-meal deals, where your entire weight is on top of the ankle. I went down in a heap. The pain shot up my leg. Watching the replay a few days later almost made me queasy. The first thought in my head was a short one: I'm done. Mark Smaha, our trainer, rushed out and helped me to my feet. I couldn't walk on the ankle. As I came off the field, Steve Birnbaum came in to replace me. His eyes were like saucers. At that point in time, he had thrown all of 20 career passes. "Just take care of the football and everything will be fine," I told him.

Mark and the orthopedic doctor inspected my ankle. It was throbbing through my head, but after a few minutes they tossed an anti-inflammatory pill in my mouth and told me a super-heavy-duty tape job might do the trick.

"Isn't it going to balloon up if you take off the old tape?" I asked.

"This will be fast," Mark replied.

I could see it swelling before my eyes and started to get that sensation where you can almost feel your heartbeat inside the swelling. When he finished the ankle, he then taped over my shoe and sock, too. I must have had a pound of tape on my leg. As I was testing it out on the sidelines, doing little cuts, Steve threw an interception. I immediately hobbled over to Coach Price and said I was fine. He looked at Mark, who gave him a half nod, half shrug. This was going to put a huge burden on the offensive line because I would be as immobile as a stone statue back there, but I knew I could make all the throws as long as the plant foot held firm. I really felt it as I backpedaled on my first pass attempt but the tape job had me standing tall, and as the game progressed the ankle didn't bother me at all.

UCLA took a 14-3 lead right as the second quarter started, and you could feel some of the energy seeping out of the stands. The leak didn't last long. We exploded in the second quarter. Michael Black took one in from 17 yards out on a misdirection play around left end that capped a long drive. Then Nian Taylor and I hooked up on a go route down the left sideline for a pretty, 57-yard TD that put the crowd into high gear. When he scored, I did a little "raise the roof" motion with my arms, which was quite the rage in those days. Normally I wasn't too celebratory when I threw a touchdown pass, but this one just seemed to demand it. It was the season opener, against UCLA, on a type of pass – the deep ball – I had literally spent hours working on with Coach Price and our receivers since spring. We missed the PAT but still had our first lead of the day, 16-14

The next four minutes belonged to defensive end Dorian Boose. He recovered a Bruins fumble and returned it nine yards to the UCLA 19, setting up my score from one-yard out a few plays later, to make it 23-14. We weren't done just yet. On the Bruins' next series, Dorian blocked a punt that Rob Meier caught and returned deep into Bruin territory. Two plays later, I hit Nian again, this time from 29 yards out, on a skinny post route, and we went into halftime ahead 30-14.

We had just concluded 15 incredible minutes and the feeling was indescribable. When I watched film of the game, I marveled at how effortless that 57-yard TD pass between Nian and I looked. I marveled because that pass took literally hours to complete, with repetition after repetition during summer workouts. Nian had a bit of a step on the cornerback and I let fly after planting the wrapped foot. It sounds pretty simple, but the reality is that the timing of his route and the arc on the ball had to be precise. Nian caught the ball in stride and sprinted to the end zone. It was one of five catches he had on the day for an eye-popping 200 yards. It looked easy. The reality is that it was the result of tedious amounts of practice. In 1996, I'd have hit that pass 2 out of 10 times. In 1997, it was more like 9 out of 10.

The second half, from a WSU standpoint anyway, wasn't so

great. Hicks scored two more TDs and Cade McNown passed five yards to Danny Farmer for another. In between, we put our last TD on the board and I must say it was spectacular. On the stat sheet, it said I threw a 78-yard touchdown pass. The reality was that I threw a five-yard pass to Chris Jackson on a slip screen and he darted and weaved the rest of the way. This was highlight reel stuff, a truly beautiful catch and run that also featured stellar blocks from Nian, Kevin, and Shawn.

Things really turned interesting mid-way through the fourth quarter. We had driven into Bruin territory but came to fourth down in that no man's land between punt or field goal. We decided to try a fake field goal. My buddy Dave Muir was the holder, which of course meant he was going to be passing the ball on this play. It didn't work. UCLA picked it off and proceeded to complete a soul-sapping drive until they came to fourth down about a foot from our goal line. There were less than three minutes on the clock. Rather than tie the game with a kick, head coach Bob Toledo decided to go for the TD. Hicks had pretty much carried the ball all the way down the field, but apparently the heat and the workload caught up to him because he wasn't in the backfield when they lined up.

Bill Doba, our defensive coordinator, spotted something – I don't know what it was – that he didn't like and started jumping up and down calling for a timeout. It was too late. The ball was snapped, and McNown handed off to Jermaine Lewis. Our down linemen barreled in low. Out of this mass of large bodies, Leon Bender just emerged, almost like he'd circled around into the Bruin backfield, and smothered Lewis. He stopped him cold. The ball was ours on the two-foot line. We still had to run out the clock

– and did just that with some pretty crafty play-calling by Coach Price – but for all intents and purposes we had just witnessed the play that would send this team rocketing toward history. Over the course of the year, you could probably point to six or seven truly season-altering plays and this was number one. Stopping a team – a very good team – at the goal line to win a game is like pouring Red Bull in your veins. We felt like we were invincible. There was no mountain we couldn't conquer.

As the time ran down on that Saturday afternoon, I took a knee, ran over to do a fist pump toward the stands where my family was sitting, and then turned around for a big embrace with Jason McEndoo, and then Steve Birnbaum. A moment later, Lynn Swann was coming up to me with a mic in his hand. This was just absolutely surreal. A Steelers fan as a kid, he was a hero of mine. Now he wanted to talk with me? Pretty soon my little brother Brady was standing next to me, telling me how nervous Mom and Dad had been. I told him I was right there with them trying to kill those final two-and-a-half minutes. Winning that game was a defining moment for us, because the year previous we had lost so many close games like this one.

My folks would reserve the hospitality room at either the Best Western or the Holiday Inn Express on game days so all our family and friends could get together, and as I hobbled in that evening after the game everyone looked at me, wondering what had happened. Mark Smaha had put me in a boot because the ankle was really swollen. As much as it ached, it was a good ache. I had battled hard and was sore, but it was a good sore, like I'd earned it.

Years later, I watched highlights of that game. As the clock wound down, the crowd noise jubilant, Keith Jackson's parting words were fortuitous: "And so ends a hot day in Palouse country, the party just beginning . . ."

THE PRICE IS RIGHT

It holds as true today as it did it 1997: Mike Price bleeds crimson. He's had it running through his veins since he was 11 years old and his big brother Geoff landed a scholarship to play for the Cougars. That was in the late 1950s and it lit a spark in Mike that has never, ever flamed out. Some people dream of being a doctor or police officer or quarterback in the NFL. Mike dreamed of coaching the Washington State Cougars.

He is upbeat and outgoing by nature, but the off-the-charts enthusiasm he displayed as head coach of the Cougars from 1989 to 2002 was obviously much deeper than that. It transcended personality or job description. For Mike, coaching the Cougars was livin' the dream. WSU is a school that "gets in your blood," as Keith Jackson once said. Old coaches like Jim Sweeney, Jim Walden, Marv Harshman and George Raveling talk about the place with a love and respect that borders on religious. With Mike, however, it's just a little different. It's more personal. More ingrained, like part of his soul. When he told recruits how special it was to be a Cougar, he had a gleam in his eyes. If you looked in them, I'd swear you'd be gazing at the kid from Everett whose older brother was knockin' heads for Washington State.

Mike followed in Geoff's footsteps, becoming a Cougar player himself in the mid-1960s. He transferred to the University of Puget Sound in search of playing time, but the Cougar spirit never wavered. In the ensuing years he would return to WSU three times – first as a graduate assistant, then an assistant coach and finally, as head coach. Pullman was always his goal. He applied for the job three times before getting it, losing out to Jim Walden in 1977 and Dennis Erickson in 1986. When Dennis was lured to Miami by Sam Jankovich, the Price was finally right.

I first "met" Coach Price in a phone call. I don't really remember what we talked about but the takeaways were pretty clear: He was personable and gregarious. I felt like there was an instant connection between us. He was fun to talk with. But as a recruited athlete you always feel like you're the queen of the ball and everyone is trying to woo you, so you never really know for sure who's legit and who's not. We first met face-to-face when he came out to Great Falls during my senior year of high school to visit with me and my parents. I remember taking him and assistant coach George Yarno downstairs to show them all the posters and trophies in my room. My mom was just absolutely mortified because you had to go through the laundry room – scattered with laundry at the time – to get there. She was so upset. It got better, though. Our dog, a Lhasa Apso named Licorice, was kind of jumping around on Coach Price's leg the whole time and rubbing up against him. That's not bad if you like dogs, but we discovered earlier that day that our beloved pooch was doubling as a flea farm, so now my mom was really worried these coaches were going to think we were a family of slobs when they spotted fleas jumping off their legs.

When we sat down in the living room to talk, I had just three questions on my mind: What other quarterbacks were in the program? Could I play right away? And could I get to the NFL by going to WSU? Coach Price answered them head on. "We are losing our senior quarterback (Mike Pattinson) and expect to have a great quarterback competition next fall," he said. "You definitely could play in the NFL by coming to WSU. Drew Bledsoe was the first pick in the draft. And we play in the Pac-10 – we have the ability to play in the biggest bowl game of the year – the granddaddy of them all – the Rose Bowl." When he left that night, I think he felt pretty comfortable, especially when I told him I'd be in Pullman in December for an official visit. I liked him a lot, because he struck me as fatherly, loyal and intense – characterizations that I would later find out to be right on target.

One of the best things about Coach Price from a player's perspective was that his door was always open. We could pop in any hour of the day if we needed to talk with him. Parents – my mom, for instance – had similar access, though my sense was that most were pretty good about keeping under the radar. I remember after the Cal game in 1997 that my mom spotted me on TV walking up to the Bears' head coach Tom Holmoe with an angry look on my face and my finger pointing at his chest. We had crushed them that day and she didn't understand why I was fired up. She called me to find out. I explained that the Bears were giving my teammates one cheap shot after another in the second half, so

I let their coach hear about it. The way I went about it was almost like I was trying to intimidate or belittle him, and it was caught by my mom. She was appalled. Of course she couldn't tell me that I needed to make amends because I would have never accepted it. I would have been defensive. So she called Coach Price. Maria, the super-woman administrative assistant for the staff, told me about it later. She remembered answering the phone and hearing a polite voice say, "Is Mike – is Coach Price available?" Maria asked who was calling. "Well, it's Marcia Leaf, Ryan's mom." Two seconds later, Mike was on the phone, and my mom gave him the run down on my bad behavior, which he hadn't seen or heard about. She wanted me to call and apologize to Coach Holmoe. Mike agreed.

So Mike brought me into his office the next day and we talked about what had happened. But here's the kicker, Mike found a way to craft the discussion so that I came to the conclusion myself that I acted badly and that I should call Coach Holmoe and apologize. Coach Price was brilliant at that kind of thing, planting ideas in a way that people would come to the right conclusion or answer on their own. My dad is the same way. To me, that's a mark of a great leader. Long story short, I called Coach Holmoe and apologized and he was really nice about it.

The relationship between Coach Price and me wasn't all master and adoring apprentice though. We used to get in each other's faces and holler back and forth. In my first start as a Cougar, at Washington in 1995, we scored a TD late in the game to pull within 30-28. We were going to go for two and Coach Price called for a quick out to the front corner of the end zone and I told him that was crazy, that it would never work. In no uncertain terms, he told me he was the coach and I was the player. His play was perfect, and as I jogged off the field with the Apple Cup now tied up, I said, "Hey, Coach, I told you it would work." That was the beauty of our relationship. We could just go toe-to-toe in the meeting room and really argue, really yell at one another, then ten minutes later, we were hugging each other. I didn't mind at all if a coach grabbed my facemask and shook it. Some players don't, but I responded to confrontation.

There was another time, when I was late to a meeting, Coach Price and I really got into it. I was late because I was doing some media interviews, and as I walked into the meeting, Coach Price said loudly, "All right, Ryan, see me after practice for your punishment for being late." *What? He's going to make me do a gazillion up-downs for interviews the school wanted me to do?* I couldn't contain myself. I had a fit. "I was doing all this media stuff for you – I'm not promoting your god-damn school ever again. I'll be in every meeting 20 minutes early from now on because I'm not doing media. I'm not talking about how great this school is anymore!"

He just looked at me, said we'd finish the issue later, and then went on with the meeting. When it was over, he kept me there and we started yelling at each other. Practice was about to start, though, so he just said "I'll see you after practice tonight." I stormed off. At the end of practice I just started walking off the field, with no intention of staying around to talk with him. The starting quarterback isn't going to be punished for doing interviews, I thought to myself. About 20 yards into my walk toward the locker room, a very firm hand grabbed me by the shoulder and ushered me over to the side where no one could hear us. "If you take your punishment right here in front of your whole team with me leading it, it will give you so many bonus points with your teammates that you'll never understand," Coach Price told me. "You do this in front of all your teammates, just like everybody else who's late for a meeting, and it will go miles and miles." My anger melted away. I never, ever in my wildest dreams thought of it from that perspective. I dutifully did my 50 yards worth of up-downs with everyone watching. And I did them with energy. This was a classic example of what made Mike such a great coach. He was intense and firm, but in a way that was caring, and that taught you a life lesson.

Coach Price always, and I mean *always*, knew what was best for me. I wasn't ready to be on center stage during my freshman year of 1994, even though we had a sensational defense and I probably could have helped a struggling offense. I needed to redshirt that season, to develop physically but also mentally because my ego was the size of Cleveland. Great Falls, the Pac-10, it's all just football, right? That was my attitude, even though there was a big clue that I had entered a strange new world: Large, sculpted bodies flying around at warp speed. But my confidence was greater than my common sense, and Coach Price knew it. In my second year, 1995, I really disappointed him because I came into fall camp unfocused and out of shape. I didn't work enough in the off season and wasn't ready to be the starter even though I'd been telling him all winter and spring that I was his guy. My focus was off leading into that season because I got into a huge fight with my lifelong best friend that ended the friendship, and my girlfriend and I were struggling with a bunch of things. I was absolutely going into camp with my head in the clouds. It became abundantly clear that junior Chad Davis, a transfer from Oklahoma and our starter from the year before, was going to be No. 1 again. It was my own fault, but my frustration was nonetheless growing by the day. Chad and I were mostly cordial with each other, but there was no love lost between us, so that compounded matters. Things reached a boiling point early on when I came in one day after lifting weights and found that the upperclassmen had taped my locker shut. I would later figure out that this was actually a compliment, but it felt like hazing at the time. I marched to Coach Price's office and literally burst into a meeting he was having with WSU athletic director Rick Dickson. I was out of control. "I'm done with this shit. I'm out of here. I'm transferring." I then turned around, walked out, went home and started making phone call to Colorado State, Michigan and a number of others. I knew in my mind I really wasn't going to transfer, but that's the way I would try to get my way – to be outlandish and act out. And maybe if I threatened that I was going to transfer, Coach Price would say, "Okay, well, we better give this guy a more serious look."

Coach Price gave me space to cool off, then made it abundantly clear that temper tantrums never amount to much good for anyone. He told me to keep working, keep grinding, and keep pushing because I had what it took to succeed. He also knew that I was an intense competitor, so he figured out ways to get me on the field. I'd of course get time at QB when the outcome was decided, but he'd also put me on the punt team in certain situations. As that season wore on, it became pretty clear that Davis was losing his way with the team and starting to test Coach Price's patience with some ill-advised audibles and sideline commentary. I could sense my opportunity was coming if I just kept grinding. I got some serious playing time in the third-to-last game and then, finally, in the last two games of the season, against Stanford and Washington, I was given the reins. And I never let go.

That '95 season taught me a lot about paying your dues through hard work and focus. While I know I could have done some good things for the team in the other nine games of that season, I don't think the long-term benefit to me personally or the program generally would have been served. That's because I hadn't learned the lesson of persistence. That season made it pretty clear that Coach Price wasn't impressed by God-given talent alone. If you were going to be the quarterback at Quarterback U, you had to earn it through preparation, commitment and focus. That frustrating season on the bench taught me a very valuable lesson. When I did finally get my chance that year, I was not only ready but appreciative. It really set the table for what was to come – and illustrated how Coach Price put individual development and long-term goals ahead of expedience or short-term benefits.

Here's another example, one that I will never forget as long as I live. My freshman season, my Aunt Vicky passed away from cancer. She was a very special person to everyone in our family. We all took her death very hard. Coach Price told me to go home and spend as much time as I needed. I returned to Pullman several days later, late on a Thursday. Now remember, I'm redshirting so it's not like I'm somebody Mike needs to worry about in the middle of preparing for one of the biggest games of the season, against No. 14 ranked Arizona and their Desert Swarm defense. Coach Price drives over to my dorm and walks me down to his car to ask how everything went and how I'm feeling. We sat there in the parking lot at Stevenson East for the next two hours, and he just let me cry and talk about my aunt. He has 122 players under him and a huge game coming up and yet there he is sitting in his car listening to me grieve for my aunt. That's the kind of man Mike Price is. My respect and love for Coach Price is captured best by these two facts. First, he was the groomsman at my wedding – albeit an ill-fated union – back in 2001. And second, when it came time for me to pick a sports agent, I chose Leigh Steinberg and Dave Dunn because, unlike most everyone else eyeing me, they completely honored Coach Price's declaration at the start of the 1997 season that no agent would contact me in any way, shape or form until the year was over. There was one agent, from Portland, who came to town when the season was over. We were all at Mike's house talking when I mentioned my conversation with this guy earlier in the season. Mind you, I had no idea that Coach Price had asked all agents to stay away from me during the season so I didn't realize that I was unleashing some fury. Mike jumped out of his chair. He was like a mother grizzly protecting its young. He read this guy the Riot Act, and for emphasis he concluded by saying, "Now, I want you to tell Ryan right now that you knowingly contacted him against my wishes." The guy looked at me and told me that it was true. I matter-of-factly said, "You can leave, sir."

Mike was not only a father figure to me, but also my best friend. If someone was dissing him, then they were dissing me. And when I say he was my best friend, I'm not kidding. I could talk to him about anything – school, family, girls, you name it. We were totally comfortable with each other. I almost felt like a member of the Price family. I was over at their house all the time. Joyce was like a second mom to me. She would bring me pumpkin pie every Thursday night when I was watching film – a tradition that almost became like a good luck charm for us in 1997. Joyce was, and is, one of the warmest, most thoughtful people I have ever met. When I think of my four years in Pullman, she is one of the first people I think of because she was so nice to me from Day One. That was more important to me than she knows, because when you're being recruited, coaches make you think you're the center of the universe. And then when you actually get to campus and suit up, they have a job to do and winning to think about, so you go from coddled kid to one of 100 guys on the roster.

On big recruiting weekends – when a bunch of prospects were in town visiting – Mike and Joyce would have huge dinners at their house. I would always volunteer to be a player host on those weekends because it meant I could hang out at the Price house and eat the giant ribeye steaks that Mike would barbeque. He loved tending the grill. In another life, I think he would have his own cooking show. Mike loves good food and he hates to work out. He'd be a perfect celebrity chef. Being a big-time head coach is not a job for the faint-of-heart. You're always under scrutiny, the workload is basically 24/7 and the pressure, day in and day out, is immense. Having people over to the house for dinner was a pressure release for him. He loved every minute of it. And of course, the guy is as friendly and outgoing as they come, so it was always a great time for everyone.

Bar none, and that includes some great ones like Tony Dungy

and Kevin Gilbride, Mike Price was the finest coach I ever played for. He was not only a motivator and a teacher, but also a tremendous technician. In addition to being our head coach, he was also the quarterbacks' coach. He truly taught me how to play the position. I remember in my first training camp, I felt like my arm was going to fall off. Mike kept telling me – and showing me – how to throw the ball with my entire body. With foot position, hip swivel and arm angle he was fine tuning my mechanics. That wasn't just a one-time thing, either. This was an ongoing project for him. Between '96 and '97, we worked and worked on mechanics. I went into camp in '97 and I don't think I ever had a day where my arm felt like it was sore because I had learned how to throw with my body, my hips, my feet. He taught me that. When I'm working with young kids today, they sometimes look at me like I'm a technical wizard when it comes to breaking down the throwing motion. I'm not – I'm just a disciple of Mike Price's. I remember our first game in '97, at home against UCLA, I felt like I had a laser attached to my right shoulder. My ability to throw the ball down the field accurately and quickly was crazy good. I often tell Cougar fans that Mike Levenseller taught me how to read defenses and Mike Price taught me how to play quarterback.

I have a picture at home that I cherish. It shows me standing in the middle, with my mom and dad on one side, and Mike and Joyce on the other. It was taken at the Heisman Trophy presentation after the '97 season. On one side were my two anchors and role models for life, my mom and dad, and on the other was this gregarious man and his incredible wife who had guided me through four remarkable years of college. Coach Price was named "National

Coach of the Year" that season. I remember thinking at the time that the word "coach" doesn't begin to describe this man and what he means, and has meant, to so many young people. He certainly means the world to me.

FIFTY-ONE YARDS TO DESTINY
USC: 1997 Game 2

Steve Birnbaum was mild-mannered and well-mannered. I was neither. Steve was a left-hander from California. I was a right hander from Montana. He was Jewish and I was Catholic. I was older and the starter, he was a year younger and holding the clipboard. We were a true odd couple. Other than both of us being recruited by Washington State and Colorado State, there wasn't much common ground between us. Yet we clicked right from the get go. I was so comfortable with Steve that whenever Coach Price bawled me out for changing a play he didn't want changed, I'd point to Steve and say, "I'm just running what Birnie's signaling in." Steve went along with that ploy three or four times before setting the record straight.

When Steve signed with Washington State out of Chino Hills, Calif., in 1995 I vowed to take him under my wing the way Shawn Deeds did with me when I arrived on campus the year before. Shawn was a fourth-year junior when I was a freshman and he went out of his way to make me feel welcome and help me understand how the system worked. He smoothed my transition. I might have taken that goodwill for granted at the time, but because I'd received a fairly cool reception from another quarterback on the team, starter Chad Davis, Shawn's kindness really stood out.

So when Birnie arrived on the scene, it was like one of my younger brothers coming to town. It helped that he was impossible not to like, and just as loyal as a brother, too. We of course spent lots of time together in meetings and practices, and generally hanging out, but we also roomed together on road trips. Somewhere along the line we started playing Sega College Football the night before games. Steve was an outstanding Sega player. And that was a problem, because I had an iron-clad superstition that I had to win before going to bed. In mid-September of 1997, on the eve of our big showdown with USC, Steve was in a Sega groove and I couldn't beat him. He said it was late and time for bed. No way, I insisted, quitting now would be disastrous for tomorrow. Superstition demanded that I win the final game of the night.

"Ryan, it's two in the morning and we have to play USC tomorrow. You need to go to sleep." I wouldn't stop until I won. I've never verified this, but I think from that point forward Steve started losing on purpose once the clock hit midnight.

I woke up early, feeling good and ready to do something no Cougar quarterback had done since 1957: Lead WSU to a win over the Trojans in the L.A. Coliseum. After our big victory against UCLA to open the season we were lucky to have a bye before the Trojans. My right leg was in a walking boot, my lip had been split open, and I was aching pretty much all over. It was a physical, emotional ballgame that took a lot out of us. Having the bye to recharge was critical. The media story from the off-season – WSU is playing UCLA and USC back-to-back to open the season – was now topic No, 1. "We've been talking about this opportunity, the chance of a lifetime, since spring. Every lap they run, every push-up they do, every ball they throw, they were doing it in anticipation of playing well against these two teams – traditionally two of the powerful teams in our conference," Coach Price told reporters about the scheduling.

During the bye week I spent most of my football time watching film of USC. We had the weekend off, so I went to visit Bryce Erickson. We had become fast friends on my recruiting trip to Miami four years earlier and had stayed in touch. Now he was living in Seattle, where his dad Dennis was coaching the Seahawks. The two of us went downtown and this really tells you how far away I was from becoming a "star" – I bought a Danny Wuerffel jersey. I loved the Florida colors and I thought of Danny, the reigning Heisman Trophy winner, in god-like terms. Accordingly, I wore that jersey religiously. To look back now, I have to laugh because Danny was basically a peer, yet I didn't see myself in his realm at all. I had six wins and seven losses on my college resume at that point. To think I'd be at the Downtown Athletic Club in New York in a few months, contending for the ultimate honor Wuerffel had won, was absolutely ridiculous.

After the shopping trip, we headed for a TV to watch Florida State beat USC 14-7. SC's two cornerbacks, future NFL players Daylon McCutcheon and Brian Kelly, actually turned my palms clammy as I watched. They were that good and I was going to have to face them in seven days. When I got back to Pullman, I was consumed by three thoughts: my fumble that cost us the win against USC the previous year; no Cougar team had won in the Coliseum in 40 years; and the Trojans just played a great game against a great team in Florida State.

Those are the kinds of thoughts that get you in trouble. Those are pressure-filled, overwhelming kinds of thoughts. Coach Price helped get me and the entire team focused on what we controlled: our preparations for the game. He said the previous 40 years at the Coliseum had nothing to do with us. This was 1997, not '67, '77 or '87. None of that history makes any difference to us, he said. We had a solid week of practices and then headed for Los Angeles on Friday. I loved hitting the road. From the airport, our buses would get a police escort to the hotel, like we were on an epic mission of national importance. And we always stayed in nice hotels, which added to the luster.

I didn't sense any pre-game jitters beyond the norm as we arrived at the Coliseum and suited up. We had a down-to-business attitude, which was a direct result of Coach Price's approach with us all week. The day was sunny and the crowd numbered a little over 50,000, including a good-sized contingent of Cougs. It was a great day for football and we opened up on fire. We led 14-0 early in the second quarter, having put together 66- and 80-yard drives that culminated with Shawn McWashington and Michael Black TDs. The Coliseum was eerily quiet. For the guys on our team from the L.A. area, who'd grown up with that annoying fight song in their ears, this was bordering on Heaven. USC narrowed it to 14-6 on a long drive mid-way through the quarter (Gary Holmes blocked their PAT), and then just before halftime we went 54 yards in six plays to go up 21-6 on a short play-action pass to Love Jefferson, who grew up about 25 miles from the Coliseum in Garden Grove. That drive had been set up by a USC fumble that Todd Nelson recovered for us.

We weren't just winning the game, we were dominating it. We were clicking on offense and the defense was playing lights out, having held the Trojans to 137 total yards in the first half. We were damn near bouncing off the walls in the locker room. The excitement didn't last long. R. Jay Soward took the opening kickoff of the second half 95 yards for a touchdown and suddenly it was 21-13 with the momentum on their side. We came to a sputtering halt on offense. We couldn't get anything going. Early in the fourth quarter I thought we had a chance for a big play on a post dig – basically a high post route that is then flattened off into a route across the middle – to Nian Taylor. This shows how good those USC cornerbacks were. Brian Kelly played me like a fiddle, leaving enough space between himself and Nian to put stars in my eyes. Nian looked wide open to me and I passed the ball about 30 yards downfield. Kelly was just waiting in the weeds. He stepped right in front and picked it off. As he returned down the sideline, I gave chase and stepped on his heel, hyper-extending my left leg and knee and flying onto the USC sideline in a pile up. Late in a tight game you don't want to be lying in a heap on the other team's sideline. It was like a rugby scrum. I was getting kicked, pushed, punched and I couldn't get up because my leg was hurting bad. Mark Smaha came running over. He looked me over and then got me back to our side for a more thorough exam. It couldn't have been much more than two minutes later that USC was in the end zone. They also made a two-point conversion, so the game was tied at 21 with a little more than 12 minutes left.

With a neoprene sleeve on to stay limber, my knee was pronounced fine. While I was kicking myself for being baited into that interception by Kelly, I also knew that we were one play away from winning. With five-plus minutes left in the game, our defense forced a USC punt and we took over at our own 18. As I prepared to go onto the field, I looked at Coach Price and said, "This is where we define our season." He didn't say anything, but nodded. Sure enough, I fumbled right out of the gate. My heart practically rocketed up my throat, but I recovered the ball and the Ghost of 1996 was vanquished. When we re-huddled I assured the guys that had been exactly how we wanted to start this drive. I threw an incompletion on the next play, so we stood at third down and 12. Finally, on the next play, we made something happen. I hit Kevin McKenzie on a crossing pattern for a 31-yard gain. That one play nearly equaled the entire output of our seven previous second-half possessions.

The breathing room felt good and it was now first down. Coach Price called for a run but when I got to the line of scrimmage USC had seven guys packed in tight. I looked left and saw a soft cushion on Chris Jackson so I changed the play to a quick hitch. As I barked the audible, USC rolled into a cover 2. When I dropped back to throw, CJ was hemmed in. I quickly turned right, to the vertical routes by McKenzie in the slot and McWashington to the right of him. Both guys were open, but Kevin just seemed to flash in front of me, in the center of a triangle anchored by Trojans, so I fired to him, almost by instinct. And I mean, I fired it in there – a little on the high side to avoid one of their linebackers.

Kevin didn't so much catch the ball as he put his right hand up to slow it down, get control and then cradle it in the crook of his arm. He did it all with one hand. Antuan Simmons, a USC safety, had an angle on Kevin after the catch, and just as he grabbed the back of Kevin's jersey at about the 24-yard-line, Shawn swooped in from the right side and obliterated Simmons with a front-side block. It was so gorgeous you almost had to cringe at its devastation. It was the type of heads up, bloody-your-nose blocking that Mike Levenseller preached to his receivers. Kevin sprinted into the end zone, untouched, for what proved to be the winning score. When he crossed, he knelt to give silent thanks. Our sideline – and the west end-zone where all the Cougar fans were sitting – was a different story. It was like a bomb had been detonated. If there is such a thing as pandemonium, this was it. And not just on the field. A friend living in Seattle told me years later that when Kevin scored he heard screaming in his apartment building and in the building across the street. In Pullman, I was told, the roof nearly elevated off The Coug while the glass bowed at The Sports Page.

Everything about the play – the way Kevin grabbed the ball with one hand, Shawn's block, the sprint with three guys in cardinal jerseys trailing – was magical. On the replays, I noticed that Kevin and Shawn were both late getting off on the snap. That's because I was late making the audible, which Kevin had to relay to Shawn and Nian on the outside. That hesitation, I think, created a split-second of confusion for the Trojans. Kevin and Shawn were maybe five yards apart when I released the ball and Chad Morton, the free safety, thought it was going to Shawn. That meant he was slightly out of position and had no chance at stopping Kevin.

In Cougar lore, I've found that play ranks alongside Drew Bledsoe's 1992 Snow Bowl TD to Phillip Bobo (which was intended for CJ Davis, by the way!) as the most memorable in a generation. At Cougar events, people refer to "the block" or "the catch" in a way that suggests you need no other information to understand exactly what they're talking about. The morning of the Rose Bowl game, Mike Sando of the Spokesman-Review put together a full-page summary of our season. At the center of it was a story headlined "51 Yards to Destiny" and a photo of Kevin bookended by Antuan Simmons' outstretched hand on his right and linebacker Chris Claiborne on his left. "Two other plays were at least as dramatic – the goal-line stand against UCLA and the overtime stop against Arizona – but neither could match McKenzie's play for historic significance," Sando wrote. He dubbed it the play of the year. I'd call it the offensive play of the year. The goal-line stand against UCLA set the course – and locked in the confidence level – for the season, while the USC catch would, to quote Kevin, "set the tempo for the rest of the year."

We had accomplished something unprecedented that day in Los Angeles. After I took a knee and the clock ran out, I sprinted toward our fans in the end zone seats. I pointed to them, to thank them for supporting us, in good times and bad, at home and on the road. When I got to our sideline, Coach Price was in tears, and covered in Gatorade. Ryan McShane, Jason McEndoo and Cory Withrow – about 900 total pounds of nasty – were rolling around on the ground like little kids. Hugging, dancing, singing the fight song – we were having a party. It was exactly what I envisioned it to be. We were 2-0 against two good teams and headed to the top 20 for the first time since 1994.

I was almost out of my mind with joy. I was quoted as yelling, as I ran up the tunnel into the locker room, "Who's the only quarterback to beat USC in the Coliseum?" That's egotistical of course, and pretty embarrassing in retrospect, but it spoke to how truly proud I was of myself and our team. As we prepared to board the bus back to the airport and the flight home, my family was waiting with smiles as wide as Montana. I wish I had a picture because it was a sight to warm the heart. My dad and I hugged and he said, "proud of you, Son." That was a cap to a beautiful day. I always wanted to shine in my dad's eyes, so there were really no words I liked hearing more. I climbed onto the bus, hobbling a little bit from the knee, but bursting with energy. I didn't know exactly where this journey was going to end but I had no doubt it was going to be special.

THE PROFESSOR TAKES ON A PUPIL

The smell of coffee poured out like it was coming from a blast furnace. It couldn't have been any worse in a Maxwell House roasting plant. For some, the smell of coffee is even better than the coffee itself. To me, it causes damn near a gag reflex. I don't know why, it just does. So my excitement at getting permission from receivers coach Mike Levenseller to watch him break down film of an upcoming opponent was dampened by the realization that Levy was a coffee junkie. I still get a touch queasy thinking about those first moments in his office in the fall of 1994. The walls seemed to be belching fumes of java. Levy can put down ungodly amounts of coffee. He should just hook up his arm to an IV and do away with the hassle of having to pick up a mug. Levy had a deviated septum, which I didn't know about at the time, so he'd sometimes do these big sniffs – almost snorts – while watching film. I thought to myself 'this guy is going to keel over right in front of me and die from all that brown sludge he's putting into his body.'

Levy's office was small and dingy, tucked away in the rafters of Bohler Gym. The walls were gray and the air muggy. To get up there, you climbed narrow stairs to an even narrower hallway that required ducking to get through because the ceiling followed the sloped roofline. Inside, there were a few scattered chairs and an ancient TV on rollers hooked up to a Beta machine – a Beta machine! There was no diagramming of plays on the screen. Levy would watch the action, hit the pause button, and then use good old fashioned pen and paper to draw up ways to attack it. Even in the early '90s, this was old school stuff. In retrospect, it all fit perfectly because Levy is the personification of old school. He's no frills and tough as nails. In a lot of ways, he reminded me of my Uncle Greg – intimidating and a bit gruff, but a great human being. I knew Levy spent hours up there in the rafters dissecting defenses so I asked one day mid-way through my first season in Pullman if I could come along. "It's up to you," he said in a voice that belied his natural intensity. Levy always talked, for lack of a better word, quietly. I think that was part of the reason everyone paid so much attention when he spoke. If it wasn't quiet, you wouldn't hear him. You had to listen. It's not that he didn't talk, it's that he was so non-demonstrative when he did. Even on the sidelines in the heat of a game, he never gets too wound up. He was what you might call a controlled fire. At any rate, his "invitation" to come watch him digest film sounded less than welcoming, but as I got to know Levy I realized he hadn't been more encouraging because he wanted to see how much I really wanted it.

And so began the education of Ryan Leaf. Mike Price taught me how to play quarterback. And Mike Levenseller taught me how to read defenses.

Two chairs, side by side, devouring film. This was high livin' in the eyes of an 18-year-old kid who aspired to be the next Terry Bradshaw. At the time, I didn't know a cover 2 from a cover charge. Every Monday and Tuesday morning for the rest of my freshman season, and most Mondays and Tuesdays for the following three years, I'd watch film with Levy. I never did get used to the coffee, and hate the stuff to this day, but I get a smile on my face when I picture Levy up in his laboratory. As time went by, we got pretty comfortable with each other. Levy has a good sense of humor, heavy on the sarcasm, and used to pitch me all kinds of crap. I wasn't sure what to expect the first time I fired some playful jabs back at him, but he loved it.

On average, I spent probably four hours a week up in the rafters focused on enemy defenses. I had never dreamt of instruction like this. The subtleties and nuances Levy would spot had my head spinning. That first morning, we were about 45 minutes in when a dreadful realization came over me: I don't have a *#@$!-ing* clue how to play quarterback in the Pac-10. By the end of that first season of film sessions, though, I was feeling better. Still, it would be a long time before I'd get to put that knowledge to use in a game. As a redshirting freshman, the closest I'd come to game action was running the scout team against the No. 1 defense. As a second-year freshman the next season, 1995, I sat behind Chad Davis, who was our returning starter from the Alamo Bowl-winning team the year before. I finally got to play some quarterback late in '95 at Cal. I threw seven passes but was so nervous I wasn't reading any defenses, or completing many passes. I was just calling the plays that were being signaled in. I was so amped up I could hardly see straight, throwing the first pass so hard it was not only uncatchable but potentially bone breaking.

A week later, when Davis was deep into Coach Price's dog house, I took all but three snaps in a home game against Stanford. We lost, but we put up 24 points – the first time in a month we broke 14. On my third play from scrimmage that day, I had what you might call a Luke Skywalker moment. The Stanford defense lined up in a cover 2 alignment, with the right corner playing up to jam our receiver. This was exactly what Levy – my Yoda – knew I would see at some point during the game. As I stood over center, it was almost like Levy's voice was speaking to me from the Bohler rafters, telling me exactly what to do. With the corner up like that, our film studies showed that the safety basically held his ground for a few seconds after the snap. That resulted in a little pocket of open space between the two DBs that I could hit if I took a three-step drop and threw a ball with absolutely no arc on it. I called an audible and the play worked perfectly. Chad Carpenter, our terrific receiver from Weiser, Idaho, made a sweet catch down the right sideline for an 18-yard gain. It's hard to describe the thrill I felt when Chad caught that ball. To turn theory into practice, and to have it work, sent a shot of adrenaline through my system. I've loved the game of football since I was a little kid and now to be playing at this level, with this type of understanding, was almost intoxicating. For Levy, it was just another day at the office. For me, it was magical. There was a timeout after the pass to Chad and when I got to the sidelines Coach Price cautioned me about the potential pitfalls in making a throw that allowed so little room for error. I just turned to Levy and said, "We knew we could do it."

The next week, in a thriller at Washington, I made the first of what would be 24 straight starts at quarterback for the Cougars. None of those starts would have been possible – or at least as productive – without the education I received from Levy. Before that game, during warm ups, he came up to offer me his version of a high five. He called it The Cougar Claw. Instead of slapping hands, you interlock your fingers and then clasp down hard. We did that before every single game from then on, the last one being in Pasadena on a sunny January day in 1998.

The season after that trip to the Rose Bowl, a column in one of WSU's game-day magazines said all the twists and turns that came together to produce our championship year made it seem like it was destiny. I've pondered the idea of destiny and come away with no eureka-type thoughts about it all. But I do know this, without Levy teaching me how to read defenses, I can't imagine having the goods necessary to quarterback that Cougar team to Pasadena. So if destiny is going to be part of the discussion, the place to start isn't with me or the Fab Five or the Fat Five or any of the rest of that incredible team. It actually starts a couple decades earlier with a fateful decision, by a fellow Montanan that changed the course of Levy's life – and the fortunes of WSU football. Back in 1975, Levy was a sophomore receiver for the Cougars and the head coach was Jim Sweeney of Butte. Coach Sweeney ran the triple-option veer offense, which meant the ball wasn't in the air all that often. In the final game of the '75 season, the Apple Cup in Seattle, Levy was on the sidelines talking with backup quarterback Jack Thompson about how this run-first stuff was for the birds. They decided they were going to transfer to the University of Puget Sound, where Levy's brother was playing, or maybe San Diego State. Two days later, after eight seasons on the job, Coach Sweeney resigned. He said he did it for health reasons – the fans were getting sick of him. Levy and Jack decided to wait and see who the new coach would be before moving on. When Jackie Sherrill was hired, he made it clear that the Cougs were going to start airing it out. So Jack and Levy stayed. Together, they became record-setters and All-Americans whose names are still in the books. That is what you call destiny.

In 1992, the love of WSU that was fostered for Levy in the 1970s brought him back to Pullman, as receivers coach for Coach Price. He had been coaching in the Canadian Football League for a number of years following his retirement as a player. In one of the rare interviews where he talked about himself, Levy told Carter Strickland of the Spokesman-Review that the need to be near family and friends brought him back. That need was driven by tragedy – something I didn't know anything about until just a couple years ago. Levy and his wife Allison's first baby, Kaley, died in 1990 from a rare complication following heart surgery. She was just three and a half years old. I spent literally hundreds of hours with Levy, just the two of us, in my four years at WSU and I had no idea. He's a pretty private guy and tougher than crap, too, but his heart is as wide as the Palouse. That valley between gruff and warm makes so much sense, knowing now of the real-life perspective Kaley's passing must have brought to him. You have to wonder how a blow like that affects a person's outlook. The urge to withdraw and become bitter, I think, would be immense. That clearly didn't happen with Levy and Allison. They would invite me over for family dinners with their kids, J.T. and Jordan, and I always thought Levy and Allison had a unique bond, almost like a hand and glove the way they fit. It's difficult to describe. Just a real united couple. Kaley's passing no doubt had something to do with that. It could have torn them up but instead made them stronger. To be invited into a home like that helped turn a big campus into a smaller, more welcoming place for an immature kid who hadn't really ever been outside Montana. Later in life, when I was coaching at West Texas A&M and my addiction to prescription painkillers found its way into the newspapers (and the legal system), Levy was on the phone immediately lending moral support. If that doesn't tell you something about the depth of his friendship and loyalty, nothing will.

Those two sides of Levy – tough on one side, big hearted on the other – are fitting contrasts because one thing I know about him is that he can't be pigeonholed. Take coffee, for example. He only drinks the good stuff. He wouldn't be caught dead waking up with something as pedestrian as Folgers in his cup. He also breaks form when it comes to harder forms of beverage. You might think Levy was a Rainier Beer guy through and through, but he's actually a bit of a wine connoisseur. On the football field, he's the same way – blending old school ways with modern thinking. Levy is almost like a scientist when it comes to the art of playing receiver. The number of steps required to run each route, the way hands and elbows are positioned, the lean of the body relative to the defender, the way blocks are leveled and sustained. He has geometrically dissected every facet of playing receiver. Precision doesn't even begin to describe what he teaches and what he expects of his guys. And when I say precision, I mean precision. One look at the lawn in front of his house is all you need to know about his attention to detail. The thing puts the greens at Augusta National to shame. It's so perfect you don't want to step on it. In fact, I never did. Knowing Levy, I would have gotten one of those piercing stares of his if I did.

Levy played three years in the NFL and four in the CFL, but he attributes much of his approach to coaching to Otto Stowe, his position coach at WSU in 1976. Stowe was a receiver on the undefeated 1972 Miami Dolphins and learned much of his craft from one of the all-time greats, Paul Warfield. He came to WSU as the receivers coach under Jackie Sherrill. Levy was entering his junior season, and up to that point was probably viewed more as a linebacker – he loved to hit – trapped in a receiver's body. As Jack Thompson tells it, when Stowe arrived in Pullman it was like the world opened to Levy. They were a perfect match. Stowe, like Levy, was a tireless worker who could do crazy amounts of cardio without tiring. But he also was a student of the game and expected that all his players would be too. For Levy, this was like pouring fuel on a few embers that had huge potential but hadn't really sparked yet.

Today, all these years later, the impact of it all can be seen in full view. When you combine his WSU playing career with his WSU coaching career, you have one of the giant figures in the modern history of Cougar athletics. As a player, he outlasted three head coaches and helped position a fourth (his 1977 offensive coordinator, Jim Walden) to take over. As an assistant coach, he's been alongside Mike Price, Bill Doba and Paul Wulff for the highest highs and lowest lows, all the while turning player after player into more than the sum of the parts. When Coach Price left for Alabama, he didn't ask Levy to go with him. You know why?

Because he knew the response would not only be no, but HELL NO. You often hear the phrase "Cougar Pride." For nearly 40 years, Mike Levenseller has been the walking, talking embodiment of what that means.

THE WAKE-UP CALL
Illinois: 1997 Game 3

Here's a nearly lethal combination: A long flight followed by an ungodly early wake-up, followed by a too-easy-first-play that inflates your confidence, followed by a punishing running back named Robert Holcombe. We should have had our way with a struggling Illinois team in our third game of the season. Oh, we won, 35-22, but getting there was like a day-long root canal.

After our gripping victory over USC the week before, we were ranked 19th and in Champaign to face the Fightin' Illini. ESPN2 was there to capture all the action, which had us excited. Playing in historic Memorial Stadium was also pretty exciting. This was the place where Red Grange and Dick Butkus once roamed. There was just one blemish on the picture: kickoff was at 12:30 Eastern Time. Which is 9:30 our time. Which translates to a 5 a.m. wake-up call to start the day. As the results would prove, we weren't up to playing football at 9:30 in the morning.

Based on our first play from scrimmage, however, you'd have

never guessed how flat we would be. We picked up where we left off at USC, running the exact play that Kevin McKenzie took 51 yards to beat the Trojans. The Illini rolled into a cover 2 – which means two safeties high and the opportunity to attack the middle if I can get the linebackers to commit to the run – and I knew that either Shawn McWashington or Kevin would be open in the slots down the seams. As I dropped back, I looked left to make sure the safety wasn't sniffing this out. He wasn't, so I turned my focus back to the middle of the field. Kevin was coming across into a little pocket of open space and I fired. Eight seconds and 80 yards later we were ahead 7-0.

This instant success was unfortunate, because it gave us a false sense of security. Scoring like that told us this would be a cruise-control day. For the next two-and-a half-quarters we were like sleep-walking zombies. Just before halftime, tied at 7, the Cougar defense really saved my backside after I had fumbled at our own 22 and Illinois recovered. The defense held the Illini to zero yards on three plays and then the Illinois kicker missed a 39-yard field goal try on the fourth.

I remember our linebackers were all over the field that day. The three starters, seniors Brandon Moore and Todd Nelson and sophomore Steve Gleason, combined for 29 tackles. They were quickly proving that one of the big question marks coming into the season – was there life after James Darling and Johnny Nansen? – was moot. These guys were good . . . really good. In a way, they also symbolized the unique way our team was put together.

Brandon had been a Prop 48 kid – who, by the way, was now just a few months away from graduating with a double major in criminal justice and sociology. He'd also overcome a devastating loss two years earlier when his mom, Josephine, died of a brain tumor. Todd didn't even play football his freshman year at WSU, but then walked on and steadily moved up the ranks with stellar work on special teams. Steve was all of 5-foot-11 and had planned to play for Bill Walsh at Stanford. When Walsh up and retired, his replacement, Ty Willingham, pulled Steve's scholarship offer, saying he wasn't big enough or tough enough for Pac-10 ball. Fortunately, Bill Doba had an entirely different opinion of this fireplug, who would go on to a long career with the New Orleans Saints.

As for our struggles with Illinois, Leon Bender took us all to task at halftime. It was time to wake up and get our heads in the game, he said. We didn't beat UCLA and USC to come here now and lose to a team we should be kicking back to the Stone Age. He was hot. His words were slow to sink in, though, because two minutes into the second half Illinois was leading 14-7. Holcombe, their senior back, had gone 48 yards for a score. He would finish the day with 163. The guy was just a beast – big, aggressive, and strong. Two years later he was the starting fullback for the Super Bowl-winning St. Louis Rams.

As sluggish as we were playing, there wasn't a moment all day when we started to question the outcome. Holcombe's long TD proved to be the slap in the face we needed, because we proceeded to score 28 unanswered points. Chris Jackson, Nian Taylor and Shawn McWashington each caught TD passes and DeJuan Gilmore ran one in from 21 yards.

Going into the game, some of the media in the Northwest billed this game as a chance to put me on the Heisman radar of Midwest voters. I don't think I was especially convincing. While I threw for four TDs and 302 yards, my four turnovers made me look pretty average. I was disappointed in the locker room afterward and I told reporters the unusually early start time was a lame excuse.

This game turned out to be a valuable learning exercise for us, because it proved the old adage that 'you can never rest on your laurels'. Sure, we beat UCLA and USC back-to-back, but the Illini clearly weren't impressed. What matters is what you do today and next week. Last week is ancient history. That became our mantra. It almost evolved to the point that each snap was a game within a game. All that mattered was the play at hand, the series at hand. At times when we'd struggle, going three-and-out or scoreless for a quarter, we didn't dwell on it, we'd look forward to winning the next snap. With that mentality, you always knew you were just one play away from exploding on teams. The following week we would explode early and often, with a little kerosene from an unlikely source intensifying the burn.

MIXING X's AND O's WITH XOXO's

"Women", Jim Walden once said, "cause more problems for a college football team than injuries, beer and final exams put together." That shouldn't be a surprise, since we are in fact talking about males between the ages of 18 and 22 who are going to class with, living next door to and generally thinking about females between the ages of 18 and 22.

As much as coaches and administrators would like people to believe their athletes are all about business – going to school and playing ball – the simple fact is that we're all college students first and foremost. That means the opposite sex is never far from mind. We're chasing women, dating women, trying to figure women out, etc. etc. There is no bigger distraction for a college athlete than women. Not the upcoming opponent, not the person you're battling for a starting job, not the term paper you have to write. . . nothing.

From Day One in the Cougar Nation, my attention was on three things: football, school and women, but especially women.

That's not to say I wasn't obsessed with football, which I was, but when you add up the hours spent flirting, angling, daydreaming and pursuing women, it's really pretty mind boggling. Arriving in Pullman to start my freshman year was like landing in the middle of an American Pie movie. Beautiful girls, all about my age, were everywhere. The weather of course was hot, so most of these lovelies were wearing shorts and sleeveless tops. I can only guess at the amount of ogling I must have done.

While my pulse was racing, my heart was actually in Chicago, where my sweetheart from Montana, Katherine, was starting her first year at Northwestern. We were inseparable the whole summer before we went our different ways. I just loved her to death. We tried to keep the flame burning, but at that age, that far apart, and living in the temptation haven known as college, what are the odds of that working out? Not good, though we did stay pretty close for the first two-plus years of college.

One of my strengths on the football field was my vision . . . same thing off the field. I had a wandering eye. My freshman season I met a sophomore volleyball player for the Cougs named Shannon Wyckoff. She was from tiny Bush Prairie, Wash. She was smart, friendly, athletic, tall and beautiful. I thought she was pretty darn interesting. The feeling wasn't mutual. She kept me at arm's length. I was steady as rain in my pursuit, however. She finally agreed to go on a date with me close to two years – I'm not kidding – after we first met. I was one of those "thrill of the chase" guys. The more far-fetched the quest, the harder you try. I went after her with a full court press. I wrote her letters, always signing them "Ryan David Leaf #16." I went out of my way to talk with her. Over time, we just got to be good friends, and then we started dating in such a low-key way that most people had no idea.

Now here's where Coach Walden's theory about women causing more headaches for a football team than anything else falls apart. When Shannon and I finally started dating, I became a better football player. She was an outstanding student and outstanding volleyball player – two attributes that don't happen by accident. It takes discipline, organization and hard work. Her approach to college life rubbed off on me. I quit goofing off on weekends (most of the time, anyway) and really started preparing myself to tackle my responsibilities in the classroom and on the football field. She made me a better person, and may have been the single-biggest influence in getting me focused on life.

She always said she got to "see the real Ryan," not the big-man-on-campus persona I trotted out in public. I was playing a position in football that demanded I be the leader, but I didn't really know how. I don't think she fully understood how I struggled with that, but she saw it and helped me step up.

Shannon loved my family and they loved her – *I loved her!* – but my mom knew how immature I was and told her to be careful with her heart. The old saying that 'mother knows best' is true. I cheated on Shannon a number of times. We would break up and then get back together. In one of the great horse's ass moments of my life – and God knows I've had a few – I told Shannon just before I was drafted by the Chargers that we were over because "it was just a college thing" and now I was focused only on the NFL.

Back before Shannon gave me the time of day, another incredible girl entered my life while I was back home on spring break my freshman year. Her name was Jen and she was from Fairfield, about 30 miles outside Great Falls. A friend of mine introduced us and we went to a dance club in Great Falls. I would have followed this gorgeous brunette anywhere. We danced and started talking. She must have felt sorry for me or something, because I was a sight to see at the time. I was still rail thin, had just shaved my head, and was wearing two hoop earrings so I could be hip like Chad Eaton.

She had no idea I was THE Ryan Leaf from C.M. Russell High who was now in the Pac-10, but I managed – as only I could – to convey this critical information. She was unimpressed but still liked me for some reason and we talked and talked. After that night we saw each other every day for the rest of spring break. By the time I left for Pullman, I was in love. I wrote her a letter every day of the week. I would go out of my way to make trips back home to see Jen and she would come visit me in Pullman. I was so crazy about her that once when I called her at Montana State and a guy answered the phone I hopped in my truck right then and there and drove straight to Bozeman. After two years, the long distance relationship – along with my selfishness and jealousy – proved problematic and the relationship faltered. It was very sad. Jen was always an unbelievable support to me; a wonderful friend who inspired me to be a better person than I was.

Katherine, Shannon and Jen were cornerstones for me during college. They helped me grow up and helped me to understand that "the real Ryan" is a heck of a lot more appealing than the public Ryan. I've kept in touch off and on with each of them over the years, and they all turned out to be as extraordinary in adult life as they were in our youth. College wouldn't have been the same without them, and I certainly wouldn't have been the same without them.

Fans, I think, believe the Xs and Os of football sit at the center of the players' lives. For me at least, successes on the field wouldn't have been nearly as sweet – and maybe not even possible – without the XOXOs of special people to share them with.

STUPID KICKERS
Boise State: 1997 Game 4

Back in the days when Boise State was known only for its blue turf and not the quality of its football program, their kicker – yes, their kicker – started smack talking in the newspaper. He said he hated the Cougars. He said he was going to put on a Husky hat after his Broncos claimed victory over us and that he was going to "sign a football, put the score on it, and hand it to Price."

Mind you, we were 3-0 and ranked No. 15 in the country. On the same day we were beating UCLA, the mighty Broncs of the Big West were losing to Northridge State, 63-23, but that didn't stop Todd Belcastro from mouthing off. He was a Spokane native and apparently harboring some hurt feelings that Coach Price never recruited him.

Now, as a college student playing football, fightin' words like that are taken very seriously, no matter how silly they may seem. The fact they were coming from a kicker made it even more infuriating. We weren't going to let this go by without a response

127

– a response Coach Price insisted contain the number zero. Boise State, he told us, was not going to score. Their kicker was not going to get his name in the stat box for a field goal or a PAT. Nothing.

Everyone of us walked out on that field with fire in our eyes. Belcastro wasn't the sole reason why. This was our first home game since the opener against UCLA and it wasn't a "natural" sellout. An anonymous donor bought the remaining tickets, giving them away, in order to insure a sellout. This was almost as insulting as the BSU kicker.

Whether they paid full fare or grabbed one of the freebies, the crowd was jacked up. We won the coin toss and elected to receive. That was the one and only time Belcastro stepped on the field that day – to boot the opening kickoff. Our fans had been riding him badly during warm ups and it clearly must have rattled him because the kick was basically a squib.

We proceeded to knock the holy hell out of them. On offense, we firebombed them for 356 yards through the air, and another 209 on the ground. Michael Black had a huge day rushing, while Kevin McKenzie, Shawn McWashington and Shawn Tims had big days receiving. When the day was done, we had scored 58 points.

But the goal, remember, wasn't necessarily to score a mountain of points. It was to make sure Boise State left with a goose egg. Defensive coordinator Bill Doba and his troops left no doubt about that. They were amazing. Boise State crossed into our territory just twice, and one of those times was on a fumble recovery. They gained only 115 yards and punted 13 times.

The next day, Mike Sando of the Spokesman-Review called the Broncos the Peter McNeeleys of college football. McNeeley was a boxer who said he was going to wrap Mike Tyson in a "cocoon of horror" in their 1995 fight. Tyson sent McNeeley to the canvas twice in the first two minutes of their bout before the manager threw in the white towel.

There were no white towels to be had in Pullman for Boise State. Our mission was to inflict an unadulterated beat down and we did. Perhaps it was just a coincidence that two Spokane guys – defensive end Shane Doyle and linebacker Steve Gleason – made sure Belcastro went home with his tail between his legs. Shane collected two sacks and Steve had three tackles for loss. It was the worst loss in BSU history. To put an exclamation point (or maybe a dagger) on the carnage, Leon Bender told reporters afterward, "I don't think too many people broke a sweat. I think the only reason I sweated was because I had my pads on." Classic Leon.

The moral of the story is clear: If you're going to smack talk, make sure you have the goods to back it up – or at least a large halftime lead.

I remember walking down the tunnel at the half, leading 38-0, and Belcastro was a few feet in front of me. I couldn't help myself. I absolutely berated the guy all the way to the locker rooms. I don't think I made him cry, but it was a merciless trashing. I'm actually surprised, in retrospect, that it didn't trigger a brawl. He had insulted my team, but worse, he'd insulted my mentor, Mike Price. I felt I needed to protect Mike in some way, which was silly. I should have just let it be. I must admit that the thought of a kicker riling up a team as much as he did makes me laugh every time I think about it.

We were 4-0 after this one and playing unbelievably well.

By Monday we would climb two spots, to No. 13 in the nation. Our confidence was booming and the student body was starting to dream big. There was excitement on campus, a buzz in the air unlike anything I'd experienced before.

I was drinking it all in but also a little apprehensive, like this was too good to be true. Each day, I kept reminding myself that our work was far from done. Each day I'd sit in the locker room and look up at the poster Coach Price had hung on the wall with "Washington State" superimposed in the end zone of the Rose Bowl. That was my reminder to stay focused.

Pasadena was the destination, but the next stop on the journey wasn't going to be easy: it was Autzen Stadium in Eugene and their foul fans.

THE FAB FIVE

Only one of 'em weighed over 200 pounds and just two stood over 6-feet tall. Yet all could bench press 300 pounds by the time we started the 1997 season. For most Americans, the name Fab Five probably conjures distant images of Chris Weber and Michigan basketball. For any self-respecting Cougar fan, however, there is no other Fab Five in the world than this one: Shawn McWashington, Chris Jackson, Kevin McKenzie, Shawn Tims and Nian Taylor.

They gave themselves the Fab Five moniker in between the 1996 and 1997 seasons. Each of those guys was important to our offense in the '96 season, but none was the main man in the receiving corps. That honor belonged to Chad Carpenter, a very talented young man from Idaho who caught 47 passes for us that season. Each of the other guys wanted to be the main man, and the fact none was made them hungrier. So in the off-season leading up to '97 – when Chad was off with the Arizona Cardinals – they were working their tails off in the weight room and on the practice field.

And they were tight. They were not only friends but each other's biggest fans as well. I think that stemmed in part from the fact every single one of them beat the odds to get where he was. And nothing supports that statement more this one: Not one of them was a receiver in high school. In very round-about ways, the Fab Five became what a sports writer termed "one of the most productive groups of pass receivers in college football history."

Shawn McWashington, for instance, came to WSU from Garfield High in Seattle as an all-league quarterback and all-state cornerback. Kevin McKenzie was a running back who had more than 2,000 rushing yards during his junior and senior seasons at Wilson High in Long Beach, Calif., and another 640 as a freshman at Long Beach CC. Shawn Tims came to WSU as a walk on after earning all-league honors as a running back at Vallejo High School in the Bay Area. Nian Taylor was also a running back, cranking out 1,700 yards out of the wishbone offense at Ramona High in Riverside, Calif.

But nobody had an unlikelier route to the top of the receiving mountain than Chris Jackson. He didn't even play football in high school. He was a basketball and track star who went to the University of California-Riverside to play hoops. A year later he was at Orange Coast CC, where an old friend told him he should give football a try.

These five guys ultimately made me the quarterback that I was.

I get a ton of accolades and respect for what I accomplished at WSU in 1997, but in all reality, if it weren't for the immaculate protection I received from the guys up front and the heads-up route running and pass catching of the Fab Five, nobody outside of the Pacific Northwest would have had any real idea who I was.

For much of the 1997 season we were ranked No. 15 or higher in the nation. A huge reason was those five receivers playing together as a unit. They were completely unselfish, personifying what the word "teamwork" truly means. I'm sure they all wanted to catch 80 or 90 balls, but the reality of our offense and their complementary skills was that it was going to be more like 30 or 50 balls each. They were committed enough to one another to know that limiting individual goals was beneficial for the overall success of the team. Coach Levenseller knew and understood he had a tiger by the tail with those five.

Their ability to dismantle defenses was astonishing. When you can throw the ball five yards to any one of them and watch the play turn into an 80-yard touchdown, it makes life pretty damn enjoyable. When I walked into a football game, I knew the opposing secondary would never have enough good corners and safeties to cover all five in an acceptable way. The great thing about the Fab Five was that each of them brought something unique to the offense.

McWashington, whose dad Ammon was a standout running back for the Cougars in the 1960s, was scary smart. He maybe wasn't the most talented of the Fab Five, but he was a great leader and definitely the most strategic when it came to reading defenses and understanding what we wanted to accomplish.

McKenzie and Tims were inside receivers, both quick as lightning and absolutely my life preservers when things started to fall apart. When I needed to find someone quickly or I needed somebody to take some blitz pressure off me, it was one of those two. They both did a tremendous job. I always had an ongoing joke with Kevin about what he was even doing on the field. He couldn't have been more than 5-foot-9, so I always told him he was too small to play receiver. Yet he would get himself out there in all the big defensive bodies and still be wide open. He was the one who caught my lone touchdown in the Rose Bowl game and one of my favorite plays ever, 63 Y out A Hunt.

Tims wasn't recruited by WSU, or anybody else for that matter. As Coach Levy once said, "he showed up out of the blue." It was clear he could contribute, though, and he was on scholarship by the end of his freshman year. He was mostly a special teamer at first – a punt returner – and then worked his way into a significant role in the receiving corps. He too was a huge life saver for me when things started to fall apart in blitz situations. He caught 37 passes in 1997, but he was the only Fab Fiver who didn't have a receiving touchdown that season. That bit of trivia still puzzles me. It certainly wasn't for lack of having a nose for the end zone either. Shawn returned a punt for a touchdown that season and also ran a reverse for a TD in the Rose Bowl.

Nian Taylor was the youngest member of the Fab Five. He was a junior and the rest were seniors. He caught the fewest balls that season – 21 – but he averaged a crazy 25 yards per catch. In terms of raw ability, I think he might have been the best pure receiver among the five. And it showed in the first game of the 1997 season against UCLA. He dismantled the UCLA defense by catching five balls for 200 yards and two touchdowns. He hurt his ankle late in the game, which hampered him throughout the season, but he also had huge catches in the Illinois, Arizona and Arizona State games. He was always there for the "Ryan to Nian" connection.

Then there's Chris Jackson. I hope the other four guys, plus Chad Carpenter, don't take this the wrong way, but CJ was my all-time favorite receiver, college or pro. He definitely was the most athletic and talented athlete I've ever been around. The things he could do on a football field or basketball court were eye popping. Now, Chris had his demons, he fought things spiritually and emotionally, but he found a way to combat them and channel all his energy into being a great football player – not only at WSU but in brief stints in the NFL and in a hall-of-fame-type career in the Arena Football League.

Chris' ability to focus was never better displayed than in the final game of the 1997 regular season. At the beginning of the week, he told everybody that we were going to beat the Huskies, beat them badly, and he was going to have a breakout game. And just to make sure he got his point across, he added that he didn't "have much respect for them as people or players." Coach Price, of course, was furious with him. Lo and behold, Chris went out and caught eight balls for 185 yards and two touchdowns. One of those TDs was a 57-yard catch and run down the left sideline that put us up for good, 14-7, in the second quarter. A few years ago the Spokesman-Review ranked that play one of the five most memorable in the history of the Apple Cup. Chris led the team in touchdowns that season with 11 and was my go-to guy on the field as well as off it. We developed a relationship and a friendship that has spanned more than 15 years.

When I think of the Fab Five, the first word that pops into my head is "friends." They were great friends to each other and to me. I love those guys. Two other words also come to mind: selfless and persistent. For them, personal sacrifice for the greater good was first and foremost. That mentality, I think, was borne out of the fact each of these guys really had to work to get where he wanted to go. None was highly recruited or even a receiver. Yet when all was said and done, they were at center stage when 67 years of Rose Bowl frustration came to an end. The Fab Five named themselves, but by the time our magical journey was over they earned their moniker many times over.

A LITTLE EXTRA YELLOW IN EUGENE
Oregon: 1997 Game 5

You can always count on Autzen Stadium for two things: Noise and bad behavior. Depending on what side of the fence you're on, Duck fans are either some of the best in the country or some of the worst. Hostile is really the best way to describe them. The fact the stadium is built right on top of the sidelines makes it worse.

We were 4-0 and ranked 15th in the country going into our fifth game of the season, against the 3-1 Ducks in Eugene. We were averaging 39 points per game and the Ducks had just scored 49 in a wild loss at Stanford, so it had all the makings of a shootout – especially when you considered that the two of us combined for 99 points in our game with each other the season before.

The Ducks had entered the era when they were solid every year, and when they played at Autzen they were almost invincible. Going into this game, they had won four straight at home, and going back a decade they had won something like 70 percent of their home games.

It was a gray, drizzly day and in the first quarter our play on the field matched. Neither team scored in the first 15 minutes and our offense was just plain bad. Part of the problem was that we couldn't hear. In the second, we took a 14-0 lead on a pair of short runs by Michael Black. The first score, a gorgeous leap over the pile, had been set up by a fully extended catch by Shawn McWashington. The second was set up by a long pass to Chris Jackson and then a 38-yard run by Michael.

In between those two TDs, a group of Oregon fans sitting in the first row behind our sideline started getting really ugly toward Michael. Some others were shooting spit wads at us, but these clowns were throwing racial slurs at Michael. I don't know if there had been an article that week in the Eugene or Portland papers about his run-ins with the law as a teenager, but these fans zeroed in on him in a big way. They were saying some really nasty, racist things and making juvenile remarks about his last name and the color of his skin. Sports can bring out the fight in people and some fans can get pretty excited and foul mouthed. We expect it and mostly tune it out. When it turns to this kind of thing, it's harder to ignore, though Michael seemed unfazed.

I sometimes like to talk about what happens at the intersection of preparation and opportunity. In this case, it's more like what happens at the intersection of internal distress and opportunity. You see, right guard Cory Withrow apparently took his hydration a little too seriously before the game and had to urinate something fierce. There was no time to get up to the locker room – and we sure as heck weren't going to risk an offside penalty with him jumping around the next time we had the ball – so some of the guys gathered

138

around him on the sidelines with towels. Once shielded from the stands, he proceeded to relieve himself in a large Gatorade cup.

This is where the opportunity presented itself. Just as Cory finished his business, the racists started spewing their nonsense again. I'd had enough. I grabbed that cup of urine from Cory, pretended like I was drinking water, and drifted closer to the stands. Wouldn't you know it, the cup started slipping out of my fingers and the contents just dumped into the laps of the fans yelling those inappropriate remarks at Michael. While it looked like Gatorade, I'm thinking the odor and warmth of it all was a dead giveaway, because these people went ballistic. They started ranting and raving and then grabbed an usher. We just looked up and laughed because what were they going to do, tell the guy that the other team's quarterback just threw urine all over 'em? Well, I suppose they could, but who the hell would have believed them? In the middle of a game? From a guy who thinks he's a Heisman candidate? Get serious.

This was one instance where my immaturity actually proved beneficial. My dad wasn't especially impressed when I told him the story. Still, to my dying day, I will say my actions were completely justified. I'm not saying I'd do it again, but at age 21 it seemed logical to take matters into my own hands. I don't remember if the "pissed off" fans left the game or just changed topics but I do know that the racist commentary ended.

In the third quarter the Ducks kicked a field goal and then Kevin McKenzie and I connected on a 12-yard TD pass to stretch our lead to 21-3. The Ducks cut it to 21-13 about halfway through the fourth quarter, but we answered with a long, time-consuming drive that Rian Lindell capped with a 28-yard field goal in the final few minutes. We won 24-13. So much for the shootout I was expecting.

The thing that sticks out most about this game is how resilient and opportunistic our defense was. Dee Moronkola, our right corner, intercepted a fourth-down pass in the end zone that really took some steam out of the crowd in the second quarter. Two of the biggest guys on the team – 6-5 Leon Bender and 6-6 Dorian Boose – each deflected passes at the line of scrimmage that were caught by us – Gary Holmes getting one and Duane Stewart the other – and helped redirect the momentum. Gary also blocked a field goal in the game.

Two other parts of this game were memorable. First, all our interceptions came off starting QB Jason Maas, who was then replaced by a guy named Akili Smith, who went on to have a pretty fine career for the Ducks. The other thing that was memorable was the post-game interviews. We blasted them for being dirty and they blasted us for being dirty. Peter Sirmon, the Ducks' star linebacker, was particularly peeved at me, saying he expected cheap shots from me. As a quarterback, I have to say it's not easy to get in on the dirty side of our business. And that day against the Ducks I don't recall doing anything outside the rule book. My guess was that Peter may have been carrying a little bitterness around in his back pocket from the year before. In that Cougar-Duck game, which we also won, I saw him put a blatant cheap shot on Chris Jackson during a touchdown run by Michael Black. As I ran down the field to celebrate the score, I angled toward Sirmon and gave him a drive-by forearm to the back that must have at least sent a few snot bubbles out the other side.

There are worse things than being called a dirty quarterback. And there were far, far worse things than being called a dirty quarterback on a team that was now 5-0, with three of those wins coming against top tier Pac-10 schools, and two coming on the road. Our confidence was now unshakeable.

We had a bye the following Saturday, giving us an extra week to get ready for Cal. It was our second bye of the year, the first having come after the opener against UCLA. I think both were perfectly placed. The first one gave us two weeks to get ready for USC. This second one gave us a chance to heal up and relax at the mid-way point.

I headed home to Great Falls for a couple of days and got to see one of my brother Jeffrey's games. He was a senior at C.M. Russell, playing right corner and leading the state in interceptions. Like all of us in the family, Jeffrey was an outstanding athlete. The following year he was a basketball walk-on at San Diego State. My youngest brother Brady – who, ironically, would become an Oregon Duck six years later – was just 12 at the time. In 1997, though, he bled only crimson and followed every game like his life depended on it.

When I returned to campus, I discovered Coach Price had launched a Ryan Leaf Heisman campaign. It was wildly creative and didn't cost much. I didn't know about it until I walked into the football office and saw all the desks covered in leaves, big maple leaves, like on the Canadian flag. Mike had asked Maria Taylor, the anchor of the office, to lead a group of folks outside to collect them. Now they were stuffing their findings into envelopes and mailing them to sportswriters and Heisman voters around the country. Other than the return address on the envelopes, there were no written words in this mass mailing. . . just a leaf. I'm no marketing genius, but I thought it was about the coolest idea of all time.

THE FAT FIVE

The bond between a quarterback and the guys on offensive line is hard to explain. In one respect, it's like five big brothers looking after one little brother. But the quarterback is the leader of the team, not a little brother, so in that respect the relationship between the line and the QB is like Secret Service agents protecting the President. Yet we're all peers – roughly the same age, doing the same things – so in that regard it's more like being a bunch of roommates whose house happens to be a stadium and whose family room is a huddle.

No extreme is considered too far to protect the quarterback. And nothing fuels an offense like a quarterback who knows – absolutely knows – he can do whatever he needs to do because the guys up front always come through. The depth of this bond, this trust between linemen and passer, is so deep that in 1996 stupidity won out over reason to prove a point. It's a tale that shows pretty clearly that the college-aged mind probably isn't fully developed yet. It was in the fall, right before camp was to start, and six of us had gone over to Moscow to watch a replay of *The Program*, a movie released in 1993 about a college football team and all the pressures that go with it. James Caan and Halle Berry were the stars. There was a scene where the quarterback was in a bar with teammates and he said, "How far would you guys really follow me? Would you lay down in traffic for me?" So the players get up and go outside to a busy street and lay down in the middle of the line in traffic. All to show their loyalty to the quarterback.

As we're walking out of the theater, I jokingly turn to the guys and say, "Hey, I'm the quarterback – would you lay down in traffic for me?"

Of course, being the bullheaded – and hilarious – bunch they were, they marched right into the middle of Main Street. I wasn't going to let them do this alone, so I marched out there with them. It was dark outside and cars were going by and I thought to myself, "This is absolutely the stupidest thing we've ever done in our lives." But down we went, lying in the middle of the street. True to form, Ryan McShane, Jason McEndoo, Cory Withrow, Bryan Chiu, and Scott Sanderson all laid in front of me so if any cars failed to course correct they would have been squashed before me. Foolish? Yes, but symbolic of the bond between us all.

That was in 1996 – long before the nickname "Fat Five" had even become an idea. In '96, it was more like "Big Scott and the Other Four." Scott was Scott Sanderson, a 6-6, 296-pound left tackle from the Bay Area who started 34 straight games for the Cougars by the time he graduated. He was smart, strong and a tremendous pass protector, always giving me great comfort on the blind side. He was named first-team All American by The Sporting News at the end of the season and went on to play for the Tennessee Titans and New Orleans Saints. He was the elder statesman of our '96 line rotation, which included three juniors (Jason, Cory and Ryan), one sophomore in Rob Rainville and one other senior in Bryan Chiu.

Sanderson was a fifth-year senior and Chiu, while new to WSU, only had one year of eligibility to use after transferring when the University of the Pacific dropped its football program. That meant there were two wide open spots to fill on the O-line heading into the 1997 season.

Injuries knocked out a couple of contenders, Mike Sage and Jon Ottenbreit. When all was said and done following spring practices and August camp, the revised line looked stout. At the tackles, we had McShane on the right and Rainville on the left. At guard, Withrow was on the right and McEndoo the left, with Lee Harrison at center.

The Fat Five was born. The actual moniker wouldn't emerge until mid-way through the season. To a man, the Fat Five was hilarious. Every one of them had a great sense of humor. Combine that with the fact they relished playing the least glamorous positions on the field and you have a recipe for a little self-deprecating parody. They weighed, combined, close to 1,500 pounds and there were five of them just like there were the Fab Five receivers. The "Fat Five" made perfect sense.

This of course added up to one problem. With a Fat Five to now go along with the Fab Five, it meant running back Michael Black, tight end Love Jefferson and I were group-less. We started calling ourselves The Three Stooges. Fortunately, it never caught on.

The "Fat Five," on the other hand, was a hit. Sports writers and broadcasters far and wide jumped on it. T-shirts were printed, featuring a design by McEndoo, who was an amazing artist. Suddenly, and unexpectedly, the unsung workhorses of the offense were in the spotlight. They deserved it, too.

Two of the five – Harrison and Withrow – came to WSU as walk-ons in 1993. And now here they were doing something that hadn't been done in Pullman in 67 years. To go from walk on to starter at a major-conference school is no easy feat. They started at the absolute bottom of the ladder. Nothing was handed to them. Saying they had to scratch and claw their way to the top is no exaggeration.

Cory, who grew up in Spokane following the Cougs, made his mark pretty early for a walk-on. He became a full-time starter as a third-year sophomore in 1995. Lee's path wasn't so smooth. He came to WSU from Bend, Oregon, looking for a chance and had been buried on the depth chart for four, long years. Even during spring ball of 1997, when the hunt for a replacement for Chiu was underway, Lee wasn't on the radar. Considering his comparatively modest size – 6-2 and 266 – that probably wasn't surprising.

Lee had a lot going for him, however. He was smart as hell (a civil engineering major) and he worked like a mule. Best of all, at least in the eyes of a quarterback, was the way he snapped the football. It was like a loaf of bread or a bag of cotton landing in your hands. It was uncanny how smoothly he could get the ball to the quarterback. Cory, who was our center in '96, was always a little rougher on the snap, and in August workouts leading up to the '97 season the two of us were having troubles on the exchange. So I asked Coach Price to give Lee a shot at center if Cory was willing to move to guard. Cory always seemed more natural at guard anyway, having started every game there in '95, and had no problem moving over.

In a scrimmage the next day, with Lee at center, our first-team offense just barreled down the field, almost exclusively on the ground. Lee was undersized, but with our two large guards on either side of him it really didn't matter. Plus, he was a master at leverage and finding angles. And just like that, Lee Harrison's four years of banging on the door, of never once giving up on the dream of playing in the Pac-10, landed him in the starting lineup.

As for Withrow, his move to guard was no big deal because he'd played there before, and the simple fact was that he was the complete package when it came to being an offensive lineman. He had size, athleticism, intelligence and a work ethic that was second to none. He has to rank as one of the top four or five walk-ons in the history of WSU. How he went undrafted by the NFL still puzzles me, but just like he did at WSU, he showed doubters what he was made of by going on to a 10-year NFL career playing a combination of guard and center.

McShane, who mostly went by Chop or Chopper, became one of my very best friends at WSU. Chopper and I had a bond I truly can't explain other than, we loved movie quotes, especially Chris Farley movie quotes, and that first brought us together and forged a friendship that would last through anything.

Ryan was huge – 6-7, 305 – and had a serious motor, but he was no elite athlete. He was one of those guys who succeeded because he maximized every shred of athletic ability he possessed. In practice sometimes, I'd look at him as if to say pick up the pace a little, man.

But come game day, he was controlled intensity, finding ways to be nasty and get the job done.

Rainville had the unenviable task of replacing Sanderson as the guy protecting my blind side. He was from down the road in Lewiston, where he had been a big star on both sides of the ball, plus a basketball and track guy. Rob and I were in the same recruiting class, which meant he was a year younger than the rest of the O-line. That one-year difference was significant in the eyes of his linemates, too. They considered Rob the kid (despite the fact he was 6-5 and 317 pounds) and he took a mountain of crap from them. It was always in good fun and Rob always rolled with it, but the fact we were in the same recruiting class gave us a special bond. That helped give me a certain comfort level on the field that never once had me complaining that Sanderson was gone. I was always very, very secure with Rob protecting my backside.

McEndoo, surprisingly, was probably the nastiest lineman out of all of them. Off the field, he was polite, articulate, friendly and mild mannered. But Holy Jesus, once the whistle blew he was in there mixing it up. He was what you'd call a Big Nasty. He would stick on you like glue until that whistle sounded and maybe a few seconds after. Sometimes in the huddle he'd look at me like I was crazy when I'd say something to get us motivated. That was because he needed no motivation. He liked to hit. He wanted to punish, and I mean punish, the opposition for having the audacity to think they could stop our backs or sack our quarterback.

The six of us had a neat relationship. I was the type of quarterback who wouldn't get rid of the ball as fast as others. I liked to stand in the pocket, hold it a little longer, maybe a split second longer, to see if I could hit that big play downfield. In doing this, I was sacked more than I otherwise would have been. Most offensive linemen would probably get pretty angry with me because these sacks are showing up on the stat sheet like they're not doing their job. The Fat Five was totally good with it. They were team players and they knew the risk and reward of my extra second holding the ball.

I also tried to take full ownership for the sacks I was causing, which proved to them how committed I was to this strategy. The fact I was a pretty big body myself also helped because they knew I could take a beating and get right back up. When the stats came back after a game showing however many sacks we gave up, I made it very clear to them that, "Hey, you allowed me to make ten throws with the potential for a huge payoff." And the stat sheet for 1997 proved it. We averaged 9.7 yards per passing attempt. That means every time we even attempted a pass we were almost getting the first down. That is unheard of. It's a conference record I don't believe ever will be broken. We averaged 493 yards of total offense per game – a Pac-10 record at the time and a school record that I think is going to be hard to beat.

The way the Fat Five worked in a game was really something to see. They were the consummate "blue collar" linemen. They didn't say much during games. They mostly just lined up, put 100 percent effort into every single snap, came back to the huddle and did it all over again. I don't recall ever – and I mean *ever* – having to bust any of them for not taking care of business.

In Corporate America, you often hear people talk about "team building," and doing things outside the normal realm of work to boost spirit. I'm here to tell you it works, and the Fat Five is proof.

Every Friday before practice, the six of us would get together for a mini game – right side of the line vs. left side. I was the QB for both sides. Poor Lee usually got left out of this, but I think he liked the time off; he had enough on his mind being the center of a team quarterbacked by me. Watching a bunch of 300-pound guys run pass patterns while being defended by other 300-pound guys is a ton (pardon the pun) of fun. We all had a blast. After a while, it was decided that they would take turns at QB and I would be a defender. I can tell you right now that the thrill of taking an interception to the house is on par with throwing a long TD pass. To outsiders, this all would have looked like goofing around. To us, it was a way to interact and relax without the pressures of the regular game. It really became something all of us looked forward to. We did it all season long and grew closer because of it.

The mere thought of the Fat Five puts a smile on my face to this day. They were hard-working characters who took their jobs seriously but didn't take themselves too seriously. For me, it was a perfect match.

THE BEST 40 MINUTES IN MARTIN HISTORY
Cal: 1997 Game 6

Chris Jackson and I became, and remain, close friends. One of the reasons why is because you always know exactly what he's thinking. Chris – better known as CJ – doesn't have a phony bone in his body. When he came home to Montana with me one time for a few days of fun before we started summer school he was just dumbfounded to see people wearing cowboy boots and hats. "You're one of them," he told me, not in a judgmental way, but in a light-bulb-turning-on kind of way.

Chris was from Southern California, and to him, Great Falls was like something out of a back lot in Hollywood. Pullman is remote, but it's a college town. Great Falls is chewing tobacco, gun racks and flannel shirts. Chris was fascinated by it. This Nike-wearing, Pac-10 quarterback by day is actually a sheltered kid from the sticks, he would tell me.

Such honesty was a CJ trait, as Apple Cup Week 1997 would later illustrate in a very public way. He always called it like he saw it. So right after we crushed Cal, 63-37, in front of a sun-drenched Homecoming crowd in Pullman, he was straight to the point when talking with the media: "This reminds me of playing back at the JC, but it felt good to come out here. . . and hook up twice with Ryan in the first half."

Nobody thought twice about the fact he just likened Cal to a junior college. We were now 6-0, and no one seemed surprised we put 63 points on the board. The Bears were bad that year. They would finish 3-8. We came in ranked 13th in the country and we had history on our side – the Bears hadn't won a game in Pullman since 1979. Plus, we were coming off a bye, meaning we had two weeks to prepare for them.

During film breakdowns, offensive line coach Lawrence Livingston and his Fat Five noticed that Cal's excellent defensive tackle, Brandon Whiting, would change the plant hand in his three-point stance depending on which gap he was planning to shoot. Cory Withrow and Jason McEndoo – our two guards – wound up calling line audibles left and right depending on Whiting's stance. That's the kind of thing that can change the whole complexion of a game. It wasn't going to make the difference on this day, because we were so much bigger and faster than the Bears, but when you look at the narrow difference that usually separates a good season from a great one or a mediocre one from a good one, it's often this small stuff that fans never see.

Things started off a little shaky for us in this one, though, as Cal drove 85 yards in nine plays to take a 6-0 lead (they missed the PAT). Twenty-five minutes later, matters were back under control. We walked into halftime with a 42-6 lead. CJ and I connected on TD passes of 72 and 14 yards within a span of less than two minutes. I also teamed up with Kevin McKenzie for a 57-yard scoring strike. Things were just as good on the ground. Michael Black had TD runs of 24 and 28 yards and DeJuan Gilmore had another that covered 54.

We opened the third quarter with what I consider one of the prettiest plays ever at WSU. On second down, I dropped back to pass. Whiting had sneaked through the line and grabbed hold of my jersey and shoulder pads. I managed to shake him off, rolled right and found my outlet man, Michael Black. I made the short pass to him and then watched as he turned in one of the most amazing runs after a catch that I've ever seen. He dipped. He ducked. He dodged. He moved in and out of defensive players, and received great blocks downfield. At about the five-yard line, he eluded three tacklers and dove into the end zone. The crowd, which had been loud all day, went absolutely berserk. The play covered 55 yards.

A short time later, Nian Taylor and I went long for a 43-yard TD pass that put us up 56-6 and ended my day with 305 yards and five TDs. I'd learn on Sunday that I was now No. 1 in the nation in pass efficiency. As nice as it was to score so many points, I felt we could have executed better. I also wanted the final score, 63-37, to reflect the size of the beat down, and letting them score 31 – meaningless, yes, but 31 nonetheless – in the second half made it look too close for my taste.

In the ensuing days I would change my tune on that, because Coach Price's decision to fully empty the bench had lasting, positive repercussions. Guys who normally didn't see much, if any, action on Saturdays got a chance in a Pac-10 game. This wasn't

Boise State. It was the Pac-10 and the playing time was significant – all of the fourth quarter and part of the third was handled by back up players. That did wonders for morale. Everyone has a role on a team, some bigger than others, but there really is nothing like being on the field when the "live bullets" are being fired. Athletes want to compete and any chance to get on the field, at any age or any level, is like a shot in the arm. I remember in 1995, my second year in the program, I got to practice a little bit as a receiver in certain goal-line formations. Coach Price did this because he knew how important it was to keep me chasing the carrot. When he put me in at wide-out against Oregon that season it was like tasting sugar for the first time.

So this blowout of Cal was especially important to the psyche of the team – all 120 members. Steve Birnbaum, my good friend and understudy, scored his first collegiate TD that day on a short run. I was so excited that I ran onto the field and tackled him. That show of emotion drew a 15-yard penalty. I didn't care. I was caught up in the moment. Steve, who was in his third year with the program, was a hard worker and great teammate. He deserved time on center stage.

Coach Price called the first 40 minutes of the game the best football ever played in Martin Stadium. Tom Holmoe, Cal's coach, said there was no doubt in his mind that the Apple Cup was going to decide the Pac-10 champion. The Pac-10 race had narrowed down to the two of us at the top, with Arizona State and UCLA close behind.

A few days after beating Cal, I was asked what I thought of comments coming out of Seattle about the Huskies thinking they had a shot at the national title, even though they'd lost to Nebraska early in the season. I wasn't very politically correct in my response. "They should think about a new team in Corvallis that's going to give them fits this week. They should worry about the next game instead of what they can do to win a national championship. That's just the type of team that is, I guess, and the way they're coached."

Nothing like getting the fireworks started a little early.

MR. SIX-ONE-NINE

In so many ways, Leon Bender was the walking – and certainly talking – metaphor for our team. He got here in a round-about way, through sheer perseverance.

To know Leon was to love Leon. He was charismatic and free-spirited, always going 120 miles an hour. On the football field, he was a tornado in shoulder pads. Jim Moore of the Seattle Post-Intelligencer once described him this way, "He has a smile that lights up a room and an overhand right that darkens them." That summed up Leon to a tee.

I remember the first time I ever really met him. I was in the Cougar weight room and heard his voice bellowing at the top of his lungs, "Six-one-nine, six-one-nine, six-one-nine." I didn't understand what the hell that meant. I found out later, of course, that it was the area code for greater San Diego, where Leon was from, and obviously a source of motivation for him when slinging iron.

Leon came to Washington State as a "Proposition 48" athlete, meaning he was academically ineligible to compete his first season on campus. Mike Price was a master at finding kids who hadn't fulfilled the NCAA's core requirements coming out of high school but had the potential to succeed in college. Mike would get these guys into the system, teach them proper study skills and give them the academic support that they didn't receive in high school. Ideally, a few years later, you'd have yourself a student-athlete who was succeeding on and off the field. It didn't always work out, but Coach Price's track record was impressive.

It wasn't all smooth sailing for Leon once he got to Pullman, though. He fought hard as a freshman in 1993 to get himself eligible for the 1994 season and wound up making a contribution as a backup on the Palouse Posse. He lost his eligibility for the 1995 season, and that easily could have been the last anyone heard from Leon. But this guy was a fighter. He enrolled at Walla Walla Community College to get his grades up and it took right up to the start of the following season, 1996, to get admitted back into WSU. He had so much ground to make up that WSU didn't even include him in the 1996 media guide, which had to be on the printing press weeks before the season started. Leon started all but one game that season but his name was not to be found anywhere in the media guide.

That '96 season was frustrating because we started out so well and then lost the last four in a row – two of them, against USC and Washington, in nail-biting fashion. The Apple Cup game went into overtime. A win would have given us a 6-5 record and the possibility of being invited to a bowl game. I remember how angry Leon was afterward. Uncharacteristically, he took his frustrations out in the post-game interviews, blasting the referees and questioning the sportsmanship of the Huskies. Coach Price wasn't happy. So he decided that Leon was going to sit out the start – and maybe even the entire first quarter – of our next game, which would be the 1997 season opener. At the time Coach Price handed down this punishment, I believe we were scheduled to open against Southwest Louisiana. Over the off-season, however, athletic director Rick Dickson swung a deal to move our game with UCLA – previously scheduled for November – up to August 30th so we could get a TV payday.

Coach Price was a man of his word. While I'm sure he was kicking himself for not making Leon run a bunch of stadium stairs instead, our big defensive tackle was on the bench when we kicked off the 1997 season in front of an ABC television audience. On the third play of the game that sunny day in Pullman, Bruins star running back Skip Hicks took a trap play right over the spot where Leon normally would have been playing. Hicks took it 96 yards down to the two-yard line. What happened next was classic. Coach Price turned to defensive coordinator Bill Doba and said matter-of-factly, "All right. He's back in."

Leon proceeded to have a heck of a ball game. And with UCLA sitting 12 inches away from victory – at fourth-and-goal with about three minutes left on the clock – he smothered Bruins running back Jermaine Lewis as the Cougar defense poured into the center of the line. Cougs win 37-34.

Now when you think about how all this transpired, going back to the Apple Cup the previous season, you might presume Leon would be a picture of political correctness in the post-game interview room.

No way. Leon was his own man and he said what was on his mind. Asked if he was surprised to see Lewis in the backfield for the fourth-down play at the goal-line instead of Hicks, he loaded up and fired.

"He had taken himself out of the game. I guess that's how they do it at UCLA with their All-Americans . . . UCLA is out there in Westwood, out there in Hollywood and they don't want to work. I know a lot of people who go to UCLA and once they get there they become soft."

By the next day, the phrase, "UCLA – where All-Americans go to get soft," was on the lips of every Cougar fan in the state. I have no recollection of what Coach Price's penance for Leon was after this latest quote-making episode, but I guarantee it didn't involve sitting out the opening series of any more games.

Leon was a monster the entire season, and the honors he received afterward proved it: first-team All-Pac-10, third-team Associated Press All-American, first-team Sports Network All-American, and Senior Bowl selection.

Leon and I were good friends, but our friendship was deeper than high-fiving on the sidelines or joking around in the locker room. We were both very self-conscious young men who had a lot of confidence in what we could do on the field, but not necessarily off it. We shared a verbal bravado that was like a suit of armor hiding the fact we were still finding our footing when not standing between the white lines. Leon was much more mature than I was, as I think anyone could see by how attentive he was to his wife Liza and daughter Imani. But the shared – and hidden – insecurity made us kindred spirits.

When I think of him today, I always think of his smile. I could be in a bad mood and I'd walk into a room and see that big smile of Leon's and my day would brighten up. I can picture it like yesterday. Seeing him with a rose in his mouth after we beat the Huskies in 1997, his grin going from ear to ear, is still fresh in my mind.

Leon died in a freak accident in 1998, just five months after the Rose Bowl. He had been drafted – the first pick of the second round and 31st overall – by the Oakland Raiders and was staying at his agent's house in Georgia as he trained for the season. Leon had epilepsy, which I don't think too many people outside the team knew, and suffered a seizure. He fell and hit his head. Leon Bender, this mountain of a man with the spirit and energy to match, was dead at age 22. He had a beautiful wife and daughter. He had signed a $3.45 million contract 16 days earlier to play the game he loved. This Prop 48 kid was a success story.

And then he was gone. The shock of it took forever to wear off. When I was with the Chargers, I thought of Leon every time we played the Raiders and could almost envision his 6-5, 300-pound frame bearing down on me. Leon's mom, Antoinette, asked me to speak at his funeral. It remains one of the great honors of my life. Like everyone else there, I was mostly in a daze and don't recall much of what I said. I hope I talked about his infectious spirit, his loyalty and his perseverance, because that was what made him such a special friend and great Cougar.

Steve Birnbaum, Ryan Leaf, Dave Muir and Paul Mencke at the
LA Coliseum day before game against USC 1997.

Lippert grandparents, Ryan Leaf and Leaf grandparents

Ryan and dad John celebrate after the 1997 Apple Cup.

Back Row Parents: John and Marcia
Front Row Brothers: Brady, Ryan, Jeffrey

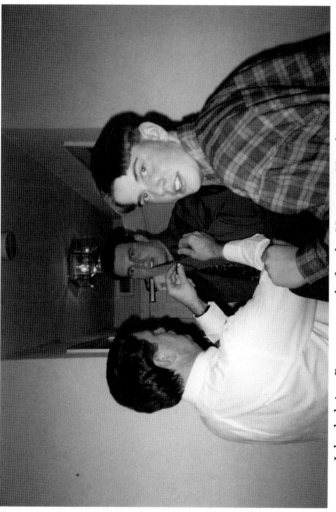

John helping Ryan get ready for the Heisman Trophy ceremony. Brother Brady looking on.

Coach Price and wife, Joyce Price with Ryan and the Heisman Trophy.

John, Ryan, Marcia before the Heisman Trophy ceremony.

Brady, Ryan, Marcia, and John with the Heisman Trophy the day after the ceremony.

THE GREAT ESCAPE
Arizona: 1997 Game 7

If anyone happened to be looking, they'd probably have thought we were nuts. Chris Jackson and I were walking up the field for pre-game warm ups, and then came to a sudden stop before turning to face each other and walking backward until we were 15 or 20 feet apart. I then reared back and fired a pass at him. He put his hands up flat and knocked the ball to the ground, clearly making no effort to catch it. Perfectly satisfied, perfectly orchestrated, he picked up the ball and we resumed our walk up field.

This bizarre little episode before our game with Arizona in 1997 might have been the difference that day.

Aw, the power of superstition. I've always had certain rituals, but when you're undefeated and ranked 10th in the country there is no tempting fate. Every possible base must be covered. For Chris and I, that meant he had to drop a pass before we started pre-game warm ups. I'm not sure exactly when or where this tradition started, but we were committed to it. We would go onto the field early, before warm ups, and play catch with an NFL football. It had to be an NFL football. Unlike college balls, the NFL balls don't have white stripes on them. That means you can see the exact spiral of the ball, with no distortion. That used to put me in good visualization mode. Somewhere along the line, during one of these pre-warm-up sessions, Chris dropped a pass, and we of course subsequently won that day's game. So now it had become critical – and I mean critical – that he drop one pass in every warm-up.

The day of the Arizona game, we were done with our private little warm-up and headed over for the start of the regular team warm up when it hit me. "Did you drop one today?" I asked. Chris hesitated for a second, then said, "No, man I didn't." We didn't even have to coordinate the next few seconds. We knew what had to be done.

The '97 season was a magical one and I wasn't going to do anything to rock the boat. That meant following a strict protocol of superstitions. After warm ups, Chris and I had to sit at midfield and say a prayer. Back in the locker room, I'd turn on a little rock – always Matchbox 20 – to get fired up, and then Steve Birnbaum and I would hit the weight room for a couple sets of bench presses to get the blood flowing and make our biceps look taut. When we were done we had to face each other and then walk backward for 20 feet. This was the way it had to be.

After our big Homecoming victory over Cal the week before, we knew destiny was on our side. We were 6-0 and now just the third team in Cougar history to be rated in the national top 10. Babe Hollingbery's final squad in Pullman, in 1942, cracked the top 10 and so did the 1958 team coached by Jim Sutherland.

Arizona was always tough with Dick Tomey's flex defense, but they were coming into Martin Stadium with a 3-4 record and were fresh off a bad loss to the Huskies, who rang up 58 points on 'em in Tucson. I figured we'd be in total control by halftime.

Four quarters after the opening kickoff, I knew for a fact there was no such thing as a gimme in Division IA football. We were tied at 34 and never once held the lead during regulation. The Wildcats found their stride against us and eventually took it all the way to a win in the Insight.com Bowl. On this chilly day in Pullman, though, bowl games became the farthest things from our minds because we were locked in a battle.

Going into the game, I felt that we could take advantage of a lot of things that they did on defense. But, they were always a little unorthodox with their flex, so you could never take anything for granted. In a story whose moral is clear – listen to your elders and follow the plan – I got us in a hole right from the start.

Each game, the first 10 plays we called on offense were all predetermined, or scripted. Coach Price did this for years and he did it for very good reasons. First, it helped calm the nerves because you knew what was coming and could prepare accordingly. And second, it gave us insight to how the defense would approach us in various situations the rest of the day. Shawn McWashington and I, feeling fat and sassy with our 5-0 record, thought we'd put a little spice into our opening series by putting a twist into the script. Unfortunately, we hadn't practiced our twist enough so when it came time to deploy it we weren't on the same page. Arizona intercepted on the third play of the game. Sixty-four seconds later they were up 7-0, and our previously amped-up crowd was suddenly silent. This was exactly the reason that the first 10 plays were scripted and why you don't try to add your own recipe to an already perfect meal.

When the Wildcats converted two long third-down plays en route to another score later in the quarter, we were down 14-0 and the crowd might as well have been in Colfax they were so quiet.

We weren't so much struggling on offense early on as we were just missing. Sure enough, just before the first quarter ended we capped a 69-yard drive with a 27-yard scoring pass to Kevin McKenzie that ranks up there as one my favorite plays of all time. I had audibled into a play called 66, which is double corners for the inside receivers and smashes – i.e. hitches to hold the cornerbacks – on the outside. Arizona's stud tackle Joe Salave'a was barreling in on me right after I took the snap, so I rolled to my left, which is not the natural way for a right-handed quarterback to roll. Now this is where you really see the benefit of years of practice and tutoring. From Coach Price, I'd learned how to really turn my hips, which meant I could put velocity on a pass without having to rely on my arm. I led with my left shoulder, turned my hips fast, and tossed a perfect, arcing dime to Kevin in the corner of the end zone – beating Chris McAlister, a future NFL Pro Bowler – for six. The intersection of preparation and opportunity never felt so good. And the crowd started to warm up, which gave us a big lift. In the second quarter, we tied the game at 14 on a straight-drop, 37-yard pass to Nian Taylor, and the home-field advantage was now back to full, vocal tilt.

Arizona rolled out a young freshman quarterback that day, who was also wearing No. 16. His name was Ortege Jenkins. He was making only the fourth start of his career. Amazingly, he had been a receiver when the season started. He played lights out against us and wound up throwing four TD passes, including one at the end of the second quarter to send them into halftime with a 21-14 lead.

Suddenly, our ship of destiny was on the rocks. When we arrived in the locker room, Dorian Boose, our outstanding senior defensive end from Tacoma, wasn't happy. Dorian was a team leader, but always in a big-brotherly type way. Not today. He was bothered and let all of us know it was time to quit screwing around. He got everyone fired up. The fact he was usually so mild mannered made the impact of his words that much stronger.

Halfway through the third quarter we tied things up, at 21, on a series that Key (Kevin McKenzie) will never forget. On third down and 13 from our own 20 he grabbed a dig over the middle for a 46-yard gainer. Three plays later we were going to pass again. When I got to the line of scrimmage it was pretty clear Arizona was going to rush six, so I tapped my helmet, which was the hot-read signal to Kevin to come across the middle rather than run a flat route as designed. Sure enough, Arizona brought six and I dumped the ball to Kevin. Almost as if designed into the play, the umpire effectively set a perfect pick on Arizona safety Dave Fipp and Kevin was off to the races for a 48-yard TD.

Arizona came right back though, and went up 28-21. We then answered with a 59-yard drive to tie on a one-yard run by DeJuan Gilmore. Both teams sputtered on their last drives of regulation and we went into overtime.

We won the toss. I passed to Chris Jackson for 13-yards on our first snap and then we kept it on the ground the rest of the way. On the seventh play of the series I took it in from one-yard out. Cougs 35, Wildcats 28. Arizona then proceeded to put together its own seven-play drive and scored on a fourth-down pass from the six.

I just assumed they would kick the extra point and we'd go into a second overtime. As a quarterback on the sideline watching the other team make the decision to go for two, and knowing that I no longer would have an impact on the outcome of the game, was very unsettling. I wanted to control our destiny. This didn't sit right with me at all. But I couldn't blame Coach Tomey. He was on the road in front of a crowd that was as fired up as any I'd ever seen, anywhere. Why not just try to win it with one play?

When Jenkins and his troops trotted back onto the field after conferring with coaches, every heart in Martin Stadium seemed to be pounding to the point the murmur was deafening. When the Wildcats broke their huddle, the Cougar Nation went absolutely berserk. Deafening doesn't come close to describing it. You couldn't have heard someone if they were yelling in your ear at point blank.

"So here it was. One game. One play. One guy," John Blanchette of the Spokesman-Review would write the next day.

Jenkins took the snap, faked a handoff up the middle that not one guy on our defense fell for and then bootlegged right, with the option of keeping it or passing. Just like in the UCLA and Oregon games, our D rose to the occasion.

Jenkins kept the ball. As he cut around the corner, Cougar safety Duane Stewart and cornerback LeJuan Gibbons were waiting to pounce. They took him down at about the two-yard-line. In desperation, Jenkins pretended to fumble the ball into the end zone, hoping for an Arizona recovery and bad officials' call. The refs didn't fall for it and Cougar tackle Gary Holmes recovered anyway. We celebrated like we had just won the Super Bowl, 35-34.

The Spokesman-Review the next morning ran a giant headline that read, "The Great Escape." I can't think of three words that could describe that game any better. There were lots of heroes for the Cougs. Our starting linebackers – Steve Gleason, Brandon Moore and Todd Nelson – combined for 26 tackles. Michael Black rushed for 116 yards. Jeff Banks punted eight times, averaging 45.1 yards. Key caught eight passes for 157 yards. And Chris Jackson not only made the crucial "drop" in our pre-warm-up warm up, but also snagged six passes for 76 yards.

To close out October undefeated and ranked 10th in the nation was pretty heady stuff. Arizona was the second nail-biting game we'd won on the season –exactly the type we were losing the year before. Our improved camaraderie and confidence in one another was making a difference that was catapulting us onto the national stage.

Ortege Jenkins was really good against us. I told reporters he was the best No. 16 on the field that day. His powers of prediction, however, left much to be desired. After the game he said we'd "get killed" when we played the Huskies a month down the road.

PLAYING WITH PAIN

It doesn't matter what the accomplishment is or what field it's in. For every person getting public recognition, there are another 10 people behind the scenes who helped make the achievement happen. Maria Taylor, the administrative assistant in the WSU football office, was one of those people who worked out of the spotlight in our run to the Roses. Sports information Director Rod Commons, now retired after a distinguished career at WSU, was one of those people. So were Judy Doba, my amazing academic counselor, and Josh Pietz, our unflappable equipment manager.

I'm not sure anyone played a bigger role behind the scenes than Mark Smaha, the director of athletic medicine at WSU for 21 years – from 1978 to 1999. He was one of those people the average Joe knew nothing about but helped put the rest of us in a position to shine. He was so talented at what he did that he's been inducted into five national and regional training halls of fame.

As players, we relied on Mark in big ways and small to either keep us healthy or to get us healthy if we weren't. Football is a violent game, so when you're in the trainer's room, it's all about me, me, me. Can you help me with this? Can you look at this for me? How soon can you get me back on the field?

Mark's office was right off the training room. Because it was so big, and because he was so cool with having us around, it basically became a player's lounge before and after practice. I don't think many of us paid a whole lot of attention to the faded photo hanging on his wall. It was a nondescript shot of a football team in white uniforms with green numbers. In reality, it was a two-ton weight on Mark's shoulders.

The picture was of the 1970 Marshall University football team – the same one made famous a few years ago in the movie *We Are Marshall* with Matthew McConaughey. Mark was the assistant trainer for the Thundering Herd back then. He was also working on his master's degree at the time, and had fallen behind on a project, so a student trainer named Don Tackett volunteered to take Mark's place for the game at East Carolina.

Marshall lost by a field goal that day. Mark had listened on the radio and then went to dinner with friends. Three hours later, State Troopers were asking him to help identify bodies. On the return home, the team plane had crashed in a gulley short of the airport. There were 75 people on board and no survivors. Mark spent the next three weeks looking inside body bags and going to funerals.

Some of our Cougar players would ask Mark about the photo on his wall and he gave a pretty basic answer about it being the worst aviation accident in sports history and how he should have been on the plane. That was it. I never gave it much thought. Mark kept it pretty much to himself – the survivor's guilt, the emotional scars from trying to identify bodies, the loss of friends and mentors. In the 1990s, the lid he'd put on it started to come off. We didn't know it at the time, but he was diagnosed with post-traumatic stress disorder. Flashbacks started hitting him at every turn. A family barbeque in the backyard would turn horrifying, as grilled chicken suddenly became the charred sight of his friends at Marshall. When we landed in Los Angeles for the Rose Bowl, the crimson-colored player bags coming off the plane suddenly turned green in his eyes and he was back in West Virginia surrounded by body bags.

Years later, when Mark had come to grips with it all and started doing inspirational speeches around the country, he told me that he once believed death and dying followed him. In fact, he had only been on the job at WSU a few months when Spud Harris, a big lineman from Tacoma, collapsed of heart failure in the middle of practice. He literally died in Mark's arms.

Mark is a caring person by nature, but the trauma from Marshall, followed eight years later by Spud Harris, put that instinct into overdrive. He liked to refer to us all as "my football players." That wasn't just a quaint phrase. He meant it. He wanted to take care of us, to protect us. We weren't just a job for him. Relationships were very important to Mark and he tended over us like we were his own children.

If we'd only known the pain and suffering that made him so hyper-concerned about our well-being.

The first time I met Mark was during my physical exam my freshman year. He struck me as a bit gruff, a bit sarcastic, and someone who knew a lot about a lot. It seemed like he was the answer man on everything I needed to know about college football and how to stay healthy. I quickly came to love and respect Mark. I was a pretty dang tough ballplayer, but when something felt or looked out of the norm, I'd get concerned. If Mark uttered four words – "You'll be all right" – then I would take it as gospel and not give the wound or twinge or whatever another thought. Years later, I found out from Mark that a few times he was a little apprehensive about telling me that, but he knew how critical those words were to my self-confidence. He truly made me feel indestructible on the field.

I remember rolling my ankle pretty severely at practice two days before our final home game, against Stanford, in '97. I hobbled off the field and Mark then carted me through the tunnel back to the training room. Well, the TV cameras caught all of it. We were two wins away from going to the Rose Bowl, so this was big, big news. My ankles were always hard to figure out because they used to swell so much more than most. Mark iced the ankle and predicted I might even be able to practice the next day, but he wanted me back in the training room at 9:00 the next morning. When he arrived home that night, news of my ankle was blaring on every TV station and his phone was ringing off the hook. That gave him a little heartburn, which would only get worse when I didn't show up for my morning appointment with him. I wanted to sleep. Besides, he told me I might be healed enough to practice – in other words, "You'll be alright" – so I had nothing to worry about. Mark was furious. He called my apartment and I didn't answer. When my roommate Dave Muir showed up that morning, Mark asked where the heck I was. "He's at home sleeping," Dave said.

Mark called me again and left a loud and very clear message on the machine. I still didn't show up, because now I was going to miss class. That afternoon I was running a little late for practice, so didn't bother to get my ankles taped before heading out to the field. Brilliant, I know.

"Why didn't you get taped?" Mark hollered when he spotted me.

"I am taped," I said.

"Well, I didn't tape you, and I was the only one who was supposed to because of your ankle."

"Well, I did it myself. I've done it a million times in high school. I just took care of it."

He was so angry with me; I think he wanted to rip my head off. He walked over, "Get your ass over here! Get on the table so I can tape you." He was mad, but he didn't let his anger get in the way of the broader issue.

"Why do you fight me so much, Ryan?" he asked.

"I don't mean to," I said.

"And why do you lie to me about stuff?" he continued.

"I don't want to get yelled at," I responded.

"Well, I'm yelling at you now and you still lied to me. What did you gain from this?"

Man, he was tough. Mark wasn't physically big but he had no fear whatsoever about getting in my face and challenging me. Even with all this guidance from Mark, I still didn't fully learn his lessons for years to come.

Mark had an uncanny way of understanding each player. We couldn't figure him out, but he always had each of us figured out.

In my case, he nailed it perfectly, once telling me, "Ryan, you are a great athlete with tremendous confidence on the field, yet very little interpersonal confidence dealing with people off the field so you try to draw attention to yourself in ways that will distract them from the truth."

Mark would do things to keep my ego in check. In stretching before practice, I always liked to do it away from the rest of the team with one of our strength coaches helping out. Mark hated this. What made me so special? There's no 'I' in t-e-a-m, right? He finally approached Gary Calcogna, the strength coach, and asked what the deal was. Gary said, "Well, Ryan asked me to." Mark politely requested that the special treatment stop.

I always wanted to do things just a little bit differently, to make myself the special one. At the midway point of practice each day, players could get re-taped or grab some ice if they weren't working on special teams. The two rules during this break from the action were that you couldn't leave the field or take off your shoulder pads unless given permission. I always liked to ice my elbow without wearing shoulder pads. One day Mark saw me icing my elbow with my shoulder pads on the ground. "You can ice your elbow with your shoulder pads on just like everybody else," he said. He was pleasant, but firm about it. With my entitlement issues, I became defensive and angry because I wasn't getting my way.

That pushing of limits by me, followed by Mark's resistance, went on for the better part of three years. I was tireless in my seemingly innocent efforts to step out of the box, but Mark never surrendered and never threw his hands up from exhaustion. He kept pointing to the boundaries. It was actually a great lesson in parenting. It was also a great lesson in getting yourself accepted by teammates.

By following the rules and expectations that applied to everyone, I was becoming a better leader. Mark knew my rebellious testing of limits was undermining my own future. If I hadn't taken his direction to heart, I'm not sure the 1997 season would have unfolded as spectacularly as it did. We were a true team. The word cohesive doesn't begin to describe it, and Mark was an important factor because he insisted that "all of us are better than one of us."

IT'S ALL IN THE TAPE
Arizona State: 1997 Game 8

I knew of him but had never played against him. Watching film in preparation for our game at Arizona State, it was pretty clear I was going to have to watch out for No. 42 on every snap. The guy was a monster. In film prep, he seemed to be everywhere, every play. He was athletic, had a nonstop motor and a nose for disruption. Once the game was underway, I learned another thing about middle linebacker Pat Tillman: He was a true sportsman. Each time he knocked me to the ground he'd extend a hand after the whistle to pick me up. I presume he did that with every quarterback he put on the turf, but I took it as a compliment that someone that good thought I was worthy of this show of respect.

That game was like a heavyweight bout. We went at it hard. At the end, Pat and I embraced. He said, "Thanks for the competition," and I told him he played a great game. When the season ended, Pat was voted the Pac-10's defensive player of the year and I was named offensive player of the year. That pairing, next to Pat, was special

175

then but it became a badge of honor for me when Pat gave up his NFL career, and then his life, to serve in the Army after 9/11.

The game that night in Tempe was one of the most exciting I'd ever played in, against a defense that had me seeing shades of the Palouse Posse. Bruce Snyder, ASU's coach, said beforehand that he thought it would be "one of the best games of the year in the Pac-10, maybe in the country."

We were 7-0 – the first time a WSU team had reached that mark since 1930 – and ranked 10th in the nation. This was our last road game until the Apple Cup. The Sun Devils, who'd gone to the Rose Bowl the season before, were 5-2 and ranked No. 20. Their defense was incredible. Up to that point, they'd only surrendered four TD passes all season.

Coach Price had been criticized for not being able to win on the road in the month of November in his time at WSU, and this game would be played on November 1. The media was all over this calendar angle. When I was asked about it, I have to admit I was quite proud of my response: "This team has never lost in November."

We had a great week of practice, and then flew to Phoenix on Friday in time for an evening walk through. It was just like our normal Friday practice in Pullman. We mess around a bit to lighten the nerves. We run our plays. The Fab Five and I decided to do a little extra work at the end of the formal practice. I was on the very far left hash and was throwing out to the right sideline. As I let one go I felt a tweak or a pop in my right elbow. At first, I didn't think much of it, just one of those sounds you sometimes hear in your joints. On the next pass, my arm was killing me. I walked into the locker room to talk to Mark Smaha, our medical director. Mark looked me over and said the best thing to do was ice it and see how it felt in the morning.

I went to bed a little apprehensive, but our game wasn't till late Saturday night. That would give me a full day to rest. When I woke up, I grabbed my pillow and tried throwing it across the room to wake up my road-trip roommate, Steve Birnbaum. The pain ran right up my arm. I couldn't even throw a pillow across a hotel room. How was I going to be able to go out and play against the best defense in the Pac-10? I was almost numb my heart was pumping so hard.

I walked into the team breakfast and asked Coach Price when he wanted to meet and mentioned that my arm was sore. I didn't tell him I couldn't even throw a pillow 10 feet. I then walked over to Mark and told him what was happening. He knew I was starting to panic. I will never forget his reply: "Don't worry – I'll figure something out. I'll fix it." He looked at Mike and gave him a little wink, and I looked back at Mike. I don't know if he could tell by the reaction on my face that I was scared to death. When I sat back down at the breakfast table, I looked at Steve and Dave Muir and said, "Both of you need to be ready because I don't know if I'm gonna be able to play." I think that shocked them, because they knew it took a team of horses to ever get me out of a game.

Mark tried a variety of treatments on the arm and it didn't feel any better. He was basically brilliant at what he did but this challenge put him to the test like no other. Like an engineer, he devised what he termed the most unique taping job of his career. He basically created a new ligament for me out of tape. When he finished, we put a neoprene sleeve over the top and I went out to see if I could throw. I could, but it was difficult. "I don't know if I'm gonna be able to do this," I told him.

He said to get good and warm and see how the first quarter goes. Once the whistle blew, I never gave the arm a second thought. Accuracy wise, I didn't have my best night, completing 24 of 49 passes, but that wasn't because of the arm. It was because ASU's defense was like a swarm of bees. The Devils stormed out to a 24-0 lead.

When I looked at the scoreboard I half expected someone to pinch me and wake me from this nightmare. This couldn't be happening. We're going to the Rose Bowl, remember? As shocking as the score was, never once did we feel like we were out of it or overmatched. Just before the half, we drove to their 22, putting us in position to throw a slant corner route to Chris Jackson. He made an amazing move at the goal line and sidestepped his way into the end zone to make the score 24-7 at halftime. That TD was like a shot of adrenalin for us.

In the locker room, I told Mark the arm was loosening up. I'd only thrown for about 50 or 60 yards up to that point but I'd made a couple good long passes. When we came out in the second half, we were a different team and I felt like I could hit anyone anywhere on the field. I had velocity on every pass. That tape job of Mark Smaha's was like something out of Star Trek. Ironically, I'd finish the night with 447 yards – more than I'd ever thrown before – and also break the school record for most TD passes in a career.

We scored 18 straight points to open the half and took a 25-24 lead when I ran for two after hitting Shawn McWashington on an

11-yard TD pass two minutes into the fourth quarter. The crowd of nearly 74,000 was stone-cold quiet. For a visiting ballplayer, that's close to nirvana.

I was so focused and intense at that point I felt like could run a marathon. There was no doubt in my mind we were going to win. It was just a matter of how many more TDs we were going to score. To their credit, the Devils didn't blink, and answered with a TD three-and-a-half minutes later. They went for two and failed so we were down by five, 30-25. The game was far from over, however. We drove to their 23 with a little more than three minutes left on the clock. On third-down, I hit Michael Black on a swing pass but he fell short of the first down by about two yards. It was fourth down and we were going for it. We emptied the backfield and went five wide. Chris Jackson was going to run a little drag across the middle. My job was to find him right away if they blitzed, and if not, to go through the rest of my reads.

They threw the house at me, rushing six. We only had five blockers. Ideally in that situation the linemen squeeze together to fill the gaps. That didn't happen. I think Jason McEndoo is still fuming at himself over it, but even if the line had tightened I'm not sure safety Mitchell Freedman – nicknamed *Fright Night* – could have been stopped. He timed his blitz perfectly and blasted through before I had taken two steps back. I ducked as he flew into me, but defensive lineman Hamilton Mee was right there, too. He gave me a shove in the back and the ball came loose. Mee snatched it up and ran 69 yards for a touchdown. The crowd went nuts. There was still 2:55 left in the game and I wasn't about to wave the white flag. We got the ball back at the 20 but on our third play I was hit from the blind side and lost the ball again. They recovered in the end zone.

We scored a meaningless TD late, on a short pass to Kevin McKenzie, to bring the final count to 44-31. Still, the margin of defeat did not reflect how good this game really was. These were two teams punching each other's face in for 60 minutes. I was angry and disappointed we let it get away. I also thought we had just blown our Rose Bowl chances. It's a long walk from the stadium to the locker rooms at Sun Devil Stadium – and the fans had rushed the field and taken down the goalposts. Watching that happen and thinking that our magical season had been taken away from us was almost unbearable. I remember sitting in the press conference talking to reporters and Coach Price taking the blame for the call on fourth down. Adding insult to injury, the Huskies were now in first place in the conference race.

As disappointing as it was, somebody got in my ear after the game and told me we still controlled our own destiny. If we won out, we'd be headed to Pasadena. That news was like pressing a reset button.

I remember Kevin McKenzie sitting next to me in the locker room, tears streaming down his face. I don't remember the exchange that happened next but Kevin – we called him Key – recalls it clearly. I told him that the only thing good that came out of this game was the TD he scored at the end because it gave me the WSU record for TD passes. While I had made strides in my maturity and outlook, that right there tells you I still had a long way to go to get out of my self-centered bubble. It actually makes me sick to my stomach now. What a complete dereliction of leadership.

After losing that game against Arizona State, all the critics came out of the woodwork again and said Coach Price couldn't win on the road in November. We took it hard. That following week of practice seemed like it went on forever. We hadn't lost a game since the overtime Apple Cup the previous year. I'm not sure any of us knew how to act with an L on our record.

Dale Grummert of the Lewiston Tribune wrote that the loss ended "the longest and most widespread fit of Cougarmania in three generations." The reality, of course, was that the party was only starting to kick into high gear.

TIME TO PAY THE EMPLOYEES

Who? What? Are you serious? As I listened to the voice on the other end of the phone, those words, along with a few expletives, raced through my mind. George Dohrmann at Sports Illustrated was detailing how I was going to be a prominent character in an upcoming cover story about a guy named Josh Luchs who wanted to "come clean" about his unsavory career as a sports agent.

This was in October of 2010 – more than a dozen years since my college playing days, so I truly had to pause for a moment and dust off the cobwebs about the who and what of Josh Luchs. I definitely didn't recall him being an agent, in part because he wasn't much older than I was. At any rate, the reporter tells me Luchs claims he paid thousands of dollars to dozens of college players around the country – including me and a few of my Cougar teammates – as an incentive for us to sign on with him when it came time to turn pro. I learn that I'm "The Whale" in Luchs' story – the big catch that will put him on the map. There's more, but that's the essence.

My head is almost spinning with all this. I told Dohrmann I'd

182

have to call him back. This was ancient history to me, someone I had not thought about in years, and a premise – that Luchs was a sports agent – that didn't ring true. I remembered him just being a friend or acquaintance of some of my teammates from California. That's how I met him in my freshman year. And I was definitely no "whale" then. I was redshirting that season and wouldn't make my first start on the field until the very last game of the following year. I don't remember much about him other than he really enjoyed hanging out with us football players. I don't recall him telling us he was an agent or even that he aspired to be an agent. He was just somebody who was quick to open his wallet. Almost like a groupie. We were young, cash-strapped and always ready for fun, so he was great to have around. Never in a million years did it cross our minds that we could be jeopardizing our eligibility or putting WSU in a bad spot.

Things escalated from picking up the tab for beer to heading down to Los Angeles on spring break and hitting the nightlife with him. One time I was in town visiting two good friends and fellow Cougar quarterbacks, Dave Muir and Steve Birnbaum, who were both from that area, and Luchs invited us to hit Las Vegas with him. Luchs paid for food and drinks, and implied that the hotel room would be covered (it wasn't). He also provided us some money for gambling, which actually turned out to be the beginning of my disconnection with him. When Luchs ran out of gambling money, he asked me to retrieve some of the cash he had given to Dave and Steve, and we got into a bit of a discussion about how he was treating my friends as afterthoughts.

From Vegas, we all headed down to Lake Havasu to stay at a

friend of my family's place. We had a fun time, but when all was said and done, I think Dave, Steve and I probably paid more for the whole trip than Luchs did. In the Sports Illustrated story he made it sound like a lavish vacation. That wasn't his only exaggeration. He also claimed to have paid off my credit card balance, and to have traveled out to Great Falls to visit with me and my parents about hiring him as my agent. This was all news to me and my folks.

My only recollection of him after the Las Vegas trip was in my rookie season with the Chargers. I got a phone call from Muir, who told me, "This Josh dude keeps calling and saying we owe him money, we owe him money and he's like stalking us." We thought ignoring him would be the best course, but then he started showing up at the Chargers facility telling me that I owed him $10,000. I can drink a fair amount of beer now and again, but $10,000 worth? This is insane, I thought. I was getting nervous though. The last thing I needed in San Diego was another distraction. Then he started telling me it was going to ruin my legacy at Washington State if my association with him became public. I was 21-years-old at the time and literally started to sweat with the idea that my accomplishments at WSU could be tarnished. So I went to the bank, withdrew $10,000 and handed it to him. It was a ridiculous amount of money but I needed him to go away. So I succumbed to what I believe was blackmail – albeit blackmail whose roots were traced to my own stupidity in college. I notified NFL security about him because I was scared to death that two weeks later he was going to show back up saying I owed him another $10,000. I never heard from him again and hadn't given him a second thought until Sports Illustrated called all these years later.

When the SI story broke, I was beyond angry – first at Luchs for twisting history, then at myself. I clearly shouldn't have been anywhere near that guy in college. The fact I was shows how immature I had been and probably even foreshadowed some of the poor decisions that were on display during my time in the NFL. The Luchs case, however, is symptomatic of a broader issue in college athletics: Many of the players have no money. Tuition, books, room and a certain amount of food are covered by your scholarship but daily living expenses that every college student faces aren't. So when a guy like Josh Luchs comes by with an open wallet, there's going to be a temptation to take advantage. And I did.

I come from a middle-class family. My mom is a nurse and my dad is in insurance. We weren't poor by any means, but there were budget pressures – especially with three boys to raise. For me, and pretty much all of my teammates, college was a time of scrimping. Aside from two pairs of jeans, my primary attire was the sweats that were given to us by the athletic department. I lived in cruddy one- and two-bedroom apartments. If it weren't for my mother and father paying the portion of my rent not covered by my scholarship, I think I would've been living on about $30 a month. I remember in our Rose Bowl year that I bounced a $13 check to Pizza Hut and asked my girlfriend's mother if she could cover it. Talk about embarrassing. Yet I had it pretty good compared to some of my teammates who came from tougher circumstances. I drove an Isuzu Rodeo with no air conditioning and many miles on it. For some of those guys, just scraping together enough money to go home for a couple of weeks in the summer was difficult. Some athletes look outside to get by, and some, who are gifted enough, leave college early to play professionally – even if they're not ready or don't want to – because of the fact they need the money.

And remember now, we are major-college athletes. That means we're basically working full-time at sports in addition to going to school. The NCAA says 20 hours per week is the maximum that players can be engaged in their sport. I'll tell you right now that if a player is serious about competing at the BCS level, he better not be limiting himself to 20 hours a week. I spent 20 hours a week just looking at film. Having a real, paying job is not possible for a student-athlete. There is no time for one. And in the summers, when there is more time on your hands, you are fully expected to stay on campus and partake in voluntary workouts and take classes so you can stay on track with the NCAA's graduation guidelines. Even if an athlete does squeeze in a summer job, he has to be very careful because it can't be construed as one gifted to you by a fan or booster.

Paying college athletes is a topic that comes and goes, but I think the time is right to do so. I say that in part because it could help neutralize Josh Luchs and the Miami-booster-gone-wild. It could stop the Ohio State tattoo parlors of the world from hitting the headlines, and maybe get Cam Newton's dad to think twice about auctioning off his son's services. I also say that simply because it's the right thing to do. These athletes are generating billions of dollars and only being paid a tiny fraction of it in the form of their scholarship. The president of the NCAA, Mark Emmert, said on PBS that it is "utterly unacceptable to . . . convert students into employees." I can understand where he's coming from, but I believe they already are employees – just ones without the benefits. These athletes have deadlines, schedules and expectations on them just like someone working in an office or factory. If they don't perform or behave properly, they can lose their job, just like a doctor, lawyer, accountant, bricklayer or garbage collector. Granted, the value of an education and college degree can't be discounted. If you look at the scholarship purely in dollars and cents, these athletes are effectively earning just $30,000 a year – and it's all non-disposable. Yet they are full-time workers generating billions of dollars.

Jalen Rose, the former basketball star and now ESPN commentator, has suggested that every student-athlete be paid a stipend of $2,000 per semester. Frank Deford, one of the great sports writers of all time, believes only the athletes from football and basketball – the sports that produce the revenue that make it possible for every other sport to be financed – should be paid. Boyce Watkins, a professor at Syracuse and one of the top advocates for paying college athletes, says it comes down to basic labor rights. He calls the NCAA "America's most powerful corporate gangsters." I don't know if I'd go that far, but I do know that when the NCAA signs football and basketball TV contracts that generate $20 billion a year, there has to be a way to put some of those dollars into the pockets of players. A stipend of even $200 a month, as Paul Wulff has suggested, would go a long way toward covering the true cost of being a college student. For a football team, in which 85 guys are on scholarship, that would add up to about $200,000 a year. That's no small chunk of change. If my math is right, that would collectively be about $24 million to cover every Division IA school that plays football.

Given the multi-billions that the NCAA earns each year, $24 million is pocket change.

Between the TV contracts, the apparel contracts, and the video games that are licensed to use the likenesses of real players, the mountain of money is a big one – certainly big enough to elevate players from the "hand to mouth" existence they now have. College football is a huge, huge cash cow. The NCAA basketball tournament produces ratings that dwarf the NBA playoffs and the Major League Baseball playoffs. I don't believe a free education is enough. These athletes are generating billions of dollars and they're also serving as the single largest marketing tool of each of their universities. The athletes deserve more. As a former player, I may be viewing the world through narrow lenses, but I know what it takes to survive and thrive in college and I know what the demands of athletics takes out of a person. To continually skirt this issue without at least giving it serious study is, to me, old-fashioned thinking that flies in the face of fairness.

GETTING BACK IN THE GROOVE
Southwest Louisiana: 1997 Game 9

We were frustrated, mad, ticked – pick any adjective you like – after losing to Arizona State and we took it out a week later on Southwest Louisiana. The Ragin' Cajuns were an independent Division IA school from Lafayette and they were struggling badly. They won just one game in 1997 and had already taken some frightful beatings before getting to Pullman, losing to Texas A&M, Texas Tech and Tulane by a collective score of 181-14.

It was pretty odd playing them in the middle of the season – actually, it was pretty odd that we were playing them at all – but this was the date athletic director Rick Dickson had swapped with UCLA in order to get that game on TV back in August.

We took our frustrations out on these guys like they were Sparky the Sun Devils. It was 56-0 at halftime. I was pulled at that point and had some monstrous stats going on because of what surely had to be the best pass protection any quarterback in the history of the game had ever received. The Fat Five were more like the Berlin Wall. An article the next day said I passed "not from a pocket but from a hotel suite surrounded by armed guards." I think I was touched – not tackled or sacked, but touched – just one time. That was one time too many for Cory Withrow. He was actually spittin' nails about it. "It's real frustrating to see him get touched when you know you can dominate a line like that," he said during interviews. That speaks volumes about the mentality that Cory and the rest of the Fat Five brought to the field each week. They strived for and were satisfied with one thing: perfection.

My goal entering the game wasn't perfection but to not come out of the line up until we had 60 points on the board. Fifty-six wound up being close enough. Besides, it gave all three backup quarterbacks – Steve Birnbaum, Dave Muir and Paul Mencke – a chance to play. It actually turned into quite the memorable day for Dave, because he ran for a TD, threw a couple of passes, returned a punt 19 yards, ran a trick play with me moving to receiver, and as the holder for placements he almost converted a muffed field goal try into a first down. He was pretty excited afterward, telling a reporter he now had a new "claim to fame" to replace the interception he had tossed against UCLA on a fake field goal.

Shawn Tims was our man of the hour. He piled up an almost unbelievable 167 yards in punt return yardage against the Cajuns, and added another 55 in pass receptions. Shawn was so good at returning punts that he was a first-team All-Pac-10 selection in 1996 and now he was rewriting the WSU record book. Speed and agility were the keys to his success but the biggest factor as far as I was concerned was his fearlessness. The guy almost never signaled for a fair catch.

The biggest highlight of the day came in the second quarter when I connected with senior tight end Jon Kincaid on a six-yard TD pass. He was the third option in my progressions but actually the true target from the moment the snap hit my hands. It was the first touchdown of Jon's Cougar career. He was a big farm boy, from the town of Palouse, and had been a promising tight end prospect coming out of Colfax High. Early in 1996 he went down with what trainer Mark Smaha called one of the worst leg injuries he'd ever seen. Jon broke his fibula, tore ligaments in half and dislocated his ankle. Not to be too graphic, but when it happened his left foot literally was pointing behind him. He was in the hospital for two weeks and then returned for another eight or nine surgeries to battle an infection. His career was basically over.

Yet here he was, a member of the greatest Cougar team in 67 years, thanks to one thing and one thing only: determination. He went through an exhaustive and painful rehab just to be able to jog, let alone play Pac-10 football. When Jon scored the touchdown that day against the Cajuns I swear every guy on our team let out a cheer.

Injuries are a part of the game we have to accept, but in the back of all our minds I think there's a little bit of "there but for the grace of God" anytime a teammate or opponent goes down. Football is a wonderful game that creates a lifetime of memories for players and fans, but it's not without cost. Jon is a prime example of what I'm talking about.

The final score that day was 77-7. Brandon Stokley was a wide receiver for Southwest Louisiana, and his father was the head coach. I remember a quote of Brandon's after the ballgame. He said, "If there's a better team in this country, then I don't know who that would be." That was about as high a compliment as you could ask for – until you compared it with his dad's. He said we were the best team he'd faced in 12 years as a head coach.

It was a great opportunity for us to showcase what we were capable of after having a really painful setback the week before in Tempe. The way we executed gave me tremendous confidence going into the last two weeks – against Stanford at home and Washington on the road – that we still had what it took, mentally and physically, to get to Pasadena.

A ROOMMATE ON A SECRET MISSION

Dave Muir holds a unique place in Cougar history. He walked on to the football team twice. The first time was out of high school in 1993 and the second was out of junior college in 1996 – albeit with a brief stop in Louisiana along the way. He was our third-string QB in 1997 and Rian Lindell's holder for field goals and PATs. He also had another role he'd never envisioned: being cruise director/social chairman/charm school teacher for Ryan Leaf. I was so awkward and uncomfortable with people off the football field that Mike Price, I would learn later, decided I needed a human interaction coach. That coach was Dave Muir.

He was perfect for it, too. The guy seemed to have a rapport with every person on campus. It didn't matter the race, creed, religion, economic status, background, you name it, Dave had a gift of finding common ground with people and running with it. Coach Price had a very astute sense of his players' personalities, their friends, and their interests. I had friends, but as the starting quarterback Coach Price believed I needed to get out more in social situations with my teammates. It would build team chemistry. With my closest confidant – Chad Carpenter – graduating to the NFL, he was concerned.

But you just can't call your starting quarterback into the office and say, "Hey, you're a social dork and need to step things up." He especially couldn't say something like that to me. With my hard head and insecurities, that would have led to psychological calamity. Instead, Mike called Dave into the office.

It was at the conclusion of spring ball in 1997. He told Dave he had a great idea: have Ryan Leaf move in with you. Dave's long-term goal was to get into coaching, and he knew Coach Price was his ticket to getting there. So, while the request struck him as a bit strange – in part, because it would mean asking his current roommate, a regular student, to move out – he felt he had no choice but to go along. As Dave would later tell the story, Coach Price just kept saying how this would be a great idea and how "he really needed to get this done." Coach didn't offer much in the way of specifics, he just reiterated that Dave should get it done. Aaron Price, Mike's son and a graduate assistant on staff, would eventually spill the beans to Dave at season's end: this was a move aimed at improving team chemistry by improving the popularity of the quarterback.

I was completely oblivious to all of this. One of my roommates at the time, Scott Sanderson, was graduating, so my living situation was up in the air. When Dave approached me about moving in with him it didn't strike me as odd. We hadn't hung out at all up to that point, but we weren't so unfamiliar that the rooming idea wasn't out of left field. I had given Dave rides home after practice and we were always in the same position meetings.

Our first month under the same roof had Dave thinking Coach Price was going to owe him lifetime employment as repayment for this favor. I was messy and Dave wasn't. I liked certain TV shows, Dave liked others. I'd play a new song so many times – two hours straight wasn't uncommon – that Dave would be on the verge of grabbing a carving knife and either putting it in my back or taking it to his own wrists.

The one thing we totally agreed on was golf. We both loved to play and we were both good. It was summer, too, so our schedules could fit it in easily. Dave turned the WSU golf course into an ongoing meet-and-greet. Mickey Long and Ryan Tujague would be with us one day, Chris Jackson and Shawn Tims another, with a dozen others in between. On and on it went, golf and cheap beer, cheap beer and golf. There also were barbeques at our place, and games of dominoes. Before long, our house was becoming Teammate Central, and when we weren't there we'd be hanging out at a teammate's house or going to a kegger. The guys started to look at me in a different light, along the lines of, "Well, if Dave likes him, he must be a pretty good guy."

By the time we started practice in August, I was at ease with damn near every man on the roster, and the socializing kept on going all through the season. My intensity and drive on the field now wasn't the only thing my teammates associated with me. I had become more human in their eyes.

And it was all because Coach Price knew Dave Muir had a gift – a gift that never appeared in the stat box or a feature story, but one that would help get this team to the Rose Bowl because the starting quarterback was now much more than just a strong arm with a cocky disposition and fire in his eyes.

In addition to being a super likeable guy, Dave was also a very good quarterback. In two seasons at Pierce Junior College he threw for 5,000 yards and led the nation in passing in one of them. There was just one problem. With cleats on, Dave was maybe 6-feet tall. He weighed 180 if you put him on the scale right after an all-you-can-eat special at Pizza Hut. He knew the game, studied the game, had an instinct for the game. . . but he didn't have the ideal body for playing in the Pac-10.

Coming out of Chatsworth High in the San Fernando Valley, he was 5-10 and weighed only 155 pounds. He received scholarship offers from places like Akron and Bowling Green, but he wanted a chance to compete at the highest level. He'd always dreamed of going to Michigan, where his parents and brother had gone to school and where his uncle had played football. The Wolverines didn't give him a look, but Mike Price and assistant coach Buzz Preston did. They liked Dave's intelligence, attitude and athleticism, so they asked him to come to WSU as a preferred walk-on.

That was in 1993. If you can't play for the Wolverines, the next-best thing is playing against them, he figured. The Cougars' first game that season was in Ann Arbor. Dave stayed with the program through the following spring but his heart wasn't in it. His sister Karen had been killed in the Northridge earthquake that January and he wanted to be back home with his family. Being stuck way down the depth chart didn't help, either, so he transferred to Pierce College near his home.

Knowing now how important Dave was to my personal

development, I'd have loved to have had him around in '94 and '95 because my ultra-competitive nature created so much awkwardness. As far back as I can remember, I was the most competitive person I knew. My mother would tell stories about how I would come in from playing wiffle ball or football in the neighborhood and be stomping mad. "What's wrong?" she'd ask, and I would exclaim, "He dropped it, Mom. He dropped the pass. I threw it perfectly to him and he dropped it and we lost the game." She would tell me not everybody takes it so seriously and not everybody is as good as you and you have to understand that. I never could.

The flip side is that my competitiveness helped me excel in athletics. But it really ostracized me. Simply put, I rubbed people the wrong way. I had some friends, but it was real work for them to hang in there with me. This was the way it was as a kid and in high school, and it's how things started off in college. Even though I was in a place where we were all very competitive, very driven people, I still couldn't deal with mistakes by others. I would get on guys in practice if they messed up and they resented that.

I look back at it now and wish I'd been more understanding and reasonable but as an 18-, 19-, 20-year- old kid, I just didn't have the maturity or perspective. Understandably, some of my teammates didn't want to follow a guy who wasn't more polished or controlled in his emotions. There's no question I was a taste best acquired over time. Part of the problem is that I think people took my in-your-face actions personally, while to me it was just part of the game. One time my backup, Steve Birnbaum, who is one of the greatest people on the planet, admonished me for my style. "When I play, I'm going to do things differently than you," he said. "I'm not going

to be the guy that's in your face and yelling and things like that."
As I replay it in my mind, I'm not even sure if it was a criticism as
much as a matter-of-fact statement about his own style.

Either way, my reply to Steve could have been better. I should
have told him that there's more than one way to lead and everyone
has to do it the way that best fits them and the people they're
leading. And that, yeah, maybe I should take a breath sometimes
before talking. Instead, I shredded him. "The bottom line," I said,
"is that everybody on this team might not like me but every single
one of them wants me to play on Saturdays. They want me on that
field, they want me being their quarterback, and they don't want
you."

Being a quarterback in the Pac-10, you don't necessarily need
to be liked, but you want to be – and need to be – respected. In
1996, my first full year as a starter, we finished 5-6 but just as easily
could have been 8-3. Maybe we lost those three games because our
team chemistry wasn't as good as it could have been, because I
wasn't the leader I needed to be.

That definitely wasn't the case going into the 1997 season. The
team was tight, very tight. And Dave Muir was one big reason why.
The fact he was even back in Pullman was one of those strange
twists of fate that tell you the stars were aligned for us. After his
stellar two years of JC ball, it looked like scholarship offers were
going to come from Rutgers, Cincinnati and Kentucky. When they
didn't, he signed with Louisiana-Monroe. He went south and hated
every minute of it – the bugs, the humidity and, above all, the
racial segregation of the community. After a couple of weeks, with
the starting quarterback's job going to someone else, he decided

enough was enough. He still had a ton of friends in Pullman from his earlier stay. One of them was Coach Buzz Preston, who had recruited Dave the first time around. Long story short, Buzz told Dave he would be welcomed back with open arms. So Dave enrolled in school and rejoined the Cougs three weeks into the '96 season. He was ineligible to play under transfer rules and knew he'd be stuck on the scout team as a fourth-year junior. But he was a ballplayer through and through. "I had to complete the puzzle I started," he would say.

Dave was far more than a social director. He was also a calming influence. As the excitement behind our '97 team grew and grew, walking to class each day became a 30-minute outpouring of attention. I was drinking it in, but Dave never let me get carried away thinking I was a rock star. I remember one time we were at practice, where I was notorious for "stealing" repetitions from the second- and third-string guys. I was just an ass about it, too. "You're not playing on Saturday – I need these reps, you don't." Dave and Steve would be furious. Dave really started mouthing off at me one day, so on one of the snaps I bypassed my receiver and fired one to the sidelines toward Dave's head, barely missing his ear. This was not a toss. It was a bullet. Dave wasn't wearing his helmet and glared at me but didn't say anything.

Later that night, I walked through the front door of our house and Dave was sitting on the couch. He started lighting me up like there was no tomorrow. "I might get my ass kicked but if you ever do anything like that again, it is going to be on," he said, putting me firmly back in my place. I felt like a scared kid. Dave had vengeance in his eyes. This was a true friend and he was so ticked off he was almost ready to come to blows over it. I told him I was sorry but the two of us hardly spoke another word for two days. I went to see Jim Bauman, the team's sports psychologist, to help get a grip on why I seemed to repel people, even good friends. There were no magic answers but at least I was a little farther down the path of self-reflection.

The night we won the Apple Cup to secure our spot in the Rose Bowl, Dave joined me and my family at their hotel to celebrate. The champagne was flowing – mostly on top of our heads. In the middle of it, with my dad standing right next to us, Dave thanked me for helping him fulfill a dream he'd had since childhood. He was a lifelong Michigan fan who grew up in the L.A. area going to Rose Bowls with his dad. Now here he was about to conclude his career in the Granddaddy of the Them All against the Wolverines. The irony of Dave thanking me in that situation has always struck me, because the plain fact of the matter is that there's a very good chance we wouldn't have been going to Pasadena if Dave hadn't transformed my relationship with our teammates. That's no exaggeration. Dave played a critical, though unconventional, role in getting us to the Promised Land. He threw all of two passes that season, yet his contribution to our success was absolutely immense. He remains a close friend to this day.

STANDING ROOM ONLY
Stanford: 1997 Game 10

So here we were, on the verge of turning the Apple Cup into one of the most anticipated contests in the history of the rivalry. All we had to do was beat Stanford in our final home game. Cardinal football was tough to figure out. They had been predicted to finish second in the conference behind Washington and had beaten Oregon State, Oregon and Notre Dame on consecutive weekends earlier in the season. They were on a four-game losing streak coming into Pullman with a 4-5 record. They were also coming with a front seven on defense – led by Pac-10 sacks leader Kailee Wong – that was really good and had me concerned.

The Cardinal linemen and linebackers weren't all that was on my mind that week. Cougarmania had reached a fever pitch. Walking to class was a love fest. Reporters and cameras blanketed our practices. To say there were off-the-field distractions would be an understatement. And then there was this little matter about my future plans. I was a fourth-year junior and having a dream season.

Should I stick around for one more year or head to the riches of the NFL? That internal debate was starting to boil inside me because if I decided to leave, then this game against Stanford would be the last I'd ever play at Martin Stadium. Talk about putting a lump in your throat. Pullman was my home. We had built something not just special, but memorable, here. Mike Price was like a second father to me.

The NFL, on the other hand, had literally been my goal since I was eight years old. It was now so close I could actually reach out and grab it. I was good enough and the way Mel Kiper and other draft pundits were talking it sounded like I was a lock-dead-cinch to go high. Coach Price kept telling me not to dwell on that, to focus on the game in front of us. It was good advice, but I couldn't follow it. If this was going to be my last game in Martin Stadium I needed to know it now, not a month from now. If this was to be my last time running through the tunnel with Cougar fans going crazy, I needed to freeze-frame it in my mind. If this was the last time I'd get to sing the fight song with my teammates inside Martin, I needed to relish every note and lyric.

I told myself that if I was going to go first or second in the draft, I was leaving. If lower, then it would be time to soul search. Given all the hype and publicity and the comparisons to Peyton Manning, it seemed fair to think being the No. 1 or 2 pick was realistic, so I prepared myself emotionally all week for this to be my final game in Pullman.

Even if this wasn't going to be my farewell, it still was going to be emotional because it definitely was the final home game for 26 of my teammates who were fourth – or fifth-year seniors. . .

twenty-six seniors. Coach Price had built this team in one of the most unique ways you'll see and the result was this large senior class. Seniors bring maturity and experience. This particular group, which featured an inordinate number of guys who had arrived the hard way, via JC ball or as Prop 48 admits, had cleared more hurdles than most. This was the foundation of the team. They oozed character, leadership and determination. It may sound trite, but this was a team and a senior class that really was destined for big things.

In addition to the impressive front seven, Stanford came into this game with weapons on offense. Quarterback Chad Hutchinson had a gun and was completing 60 percent of his throws, receiver-return man Troy Walters was a major talent, and running back Anthony Bookman was averaging over six yards per carry. "Stanford is a lot better than I anticipated, unfortunately," Coach Price told reporters. The Card had another thing going for them – momentum against us. The year before, in Palo Alto, we had jumped to a 14-0 lead then fell apart, losing 33-17. The season before, when I saw my first extended time at quarterback, we lost 36-24.

Today would be different. Not only was the stadium full, it was standing-room only – a record 40,306 packed in. As we went through final preparations in the locker room before coming out for the opening kickoff we could hear the steady murmur of our fans, almost like a herd in the distance. The marching band added the perfect touch. Just the idea of walking into that atmosphere sent shivers up my spine. When we actually did get out there, the reception was even wilder than I expected. We were their team. They were so proud of us they literally couldn't contain themselves.

Martin Stadium was more than electric, it was supercharged. This was game day on steroids.

As it had all season, our defense bent but never broke. They made one big play after another. Case in point: We had scored shortly before halftime to take a 16-14 lead but Stanford's Damon Dunn broke loose on the ensuing kickoff and looked like he was gone. Dee Moronkola was tied up with a blocker but was able to press enough to get Dunn to cut back inside. That allowed freshman Lamont Thompson to mount a mad dash and chase him down at the four. Three plays later, senior linebacker Brandon Moore intercepted a Todd Husak pass to Dunn and disaster was averted. Both Lamont and Brandon came up big all day long. Brandon had 14 total tackles and Lamont grabbed two interceptions. Dorian Boose was also lights out, sacking Husak twice and forcing two fumbles.

On offense, we started well, jumping to a 10-0 lead in the first quarter. I scored on a 4-yard QB draw, but it came at a price. Stanford's Chris Draft hit me like a battering ram as I was diving into the end zone. It felt like my shoulder had been shoved into the middle of my back. Mark Smaha checked me out, said I'd be sore, but not to worry about it. Stanford's QB, Hutchinson, wasn't as fortunate. He sprained his thumb on the second snap of the game and was done for the day, replaced by Husak.

Stanford's defense played a great game, rarely getting out of position, always keeping the ball in front of them. They played what's called a high-shell-cover-four, which made it tough to go deep. We didn't force anything and adapted, like we had all year long, to what we were seeing. I began to find Chris Jackson and

Kevin McKenzie on a steady diet of slants and digs. The two of them ended the day with a combined 16 catches for 185 yards. CJ had two TDs, both on slants from inside the 10. One of 'em was a one-handed grab.

CJ's catch of the day, however, wasn't either of those TDs. Late in the game, after Stanford had taken a 28-27 lead, CJ and I clicked on a third-and-13 pass over the middle. He was in heavy, heavy traffic but we each knew exactly what the other was thinking. When I later watched the play on film, I said to myself "That's the epitome of why we had worked so hard all summer long." He made the catch for the first down. Michael Black, who had a huge day, rushing for 174 yards on 27 carries, put us ahead for good with a four-yard TD run. We went for two and I hit Shawn McWashington in the back of the end zone to put us up 35-28. At this point the crowd was near delirious.

When the defense held and we followed up with an 11-play drive that consumed more than five minutes – ending with Rian Lindell's third field goal of the game that put us up 38-28 – the outcome was assured. A win in Seattle the following week would send us to Pasadena. As fate would have it, while we were beating Stanford, the Huskies were losing badly to UCLA so now the only roses that could possibly come out of Lake Washington were crimson.

As the seconds were starting to wind down against the Cardinal, I did something that I had seen done by many others over the years. After taking a knee, I struck the Heisman pose in front of the south grandstands. I had been cajoled into doing it by my teammates, and sure enough, I went for it. It wasn't designed to taunt Stanford.

I was just trying to give the hometown fans a smile.

The crowd went crazy. Before I knew it, the field was engulfed in bodies. People poured out of the stands, whooping and hollering. Everyone started chanting "We're No. 1" and suddenly I was hoisted into the air and being carried around on their shoulders. I remember watching Drew Bledsoe after the Snow Bowl being carried around on people's shoulders, and that memory brought me back to that moment. I said at the time that it was one of the best feelings I've ever had, and that still holds true to this day.

Peers, classmates and fans who had been so supportive all year long were carrying me around the football field celebrating what we had just accomplished. We had won every home game. We were 9-1 and flirting again with a top 10 ranking. We had a chance to be the Pac-10's representative in the Rose Bowl– provided we handled the Huskies the next week.

Amid all the chaos, I would later learn, was a more somber celebration. Fat Fivers Jason McEndoo and Ryan McShane, now two-and-a-half-years removed from the car accident that killed Jason's wife Michelle, searched for each other amid the sea of smiling Cougar fans. "Been to hell and back," Jason would say about their emotional embrace on the field. "To go out on top like this is amazing."

As we walked back into the locker room after the jubilant celebration on the field, I looked up at the superimposed "Washington State" Rose Bowl picture that Coach Price had hung in our locker room. He had placed the same poster on the wall the season before, but took it down after we lost two games in a row to fall out of the race. I was angry when he did that and told him so.

He made a point to me that it would go back when we put ourselves back in position to make Pasadena a reality. The symbolic removal of the poster made a big impression not just on me but the whole team.

After doing interviews, I walked over to my dad and gave him a big hug. "Can you believe this is happening?" I asked. A win on the shores of Lake Washington, against our nemesis, with the entire state and much of the nation watching, was our ticket to the Promised Land. The script couldn't have been written any better. The Spokesman-Review sports page the next day screamed it to the mountain tops with a giant headline, "A Nose for the Rose."

My shoulder, which had been dinged in the first quarter, was now feeling like it was hanging out of its socket, my elbow felt like it was falling off, and my ankle felt like I was a 100 years old. And you know what? I couldn't wait to plug in game film on the Huskies and then get back out on the field to prepare. Going to the NFL was the farthest thing from my mind at that point. This was all about being a Cougar. It was a glorious time to be a Cougar.

YOU CAN QUOTE ME ON THAT

So, here it was . . . the article that my parents didn't want me to see. In a corner of their basement sit box after box of mementos from my playing days, including virtually every newspaper article of significance about me while at WSU. I found this particular one, 12 years after the fact, while rummaging around one day. I was surprised my folks actually hung on to a copy. Mom and Dad and my grandparents had all been interviewed by the reporter, Julie Sullivan, and this wasn't the story they were hoping it might be.

The headline simply read "Life of Ryan." The subhead wasn't as bland: "The boy Montana loved to hate is riding high."

It was the day after Christmas, 1997, and a big splash in that day's Spokesman-Review. I was in Santa Monica with the team, getting ready for the Rose Bowl, so had no idea it had been published. Much later I would learn that the story spread quickly throughout the Cougar Nation. It totaled 2,448 words, but basically went something like this: No one in Great Falls has anything nice to say about Ryan Leaf. The state of Montana is glad he left. WSU's big star is a jerk.

Reading it in my parents' basement a dozen years later, I could see why they were upset, but having seen and dealt with far worse in the intervening years, the story wasn't all that bad. In fact, it pretty much said what was true: I was strong-willed and ultra-competitive, and it tended to tick people off. There's nothing false about that.

I think this also must have been one of the first comparisons – with literally thousands to follow – between my relative popularity and Peyton Manning's.

The week the Heisman Trophy was awarded, Tennesseans were ready to canonize Peyton Manning, and fans in Michigan cried out for Charles Woodson. The Great Falls Tribune asked Montanans who should win.

"Anyone but Ryan Leaf . . .," wrote one anonymous author. "The Heisman Trophy should go to someone who portrays a true athlete's attitude on the field or off. Those of us who went to school with Ryan could tell you what he is really like. He may be good at his game of football, but he needs work in his game of life."

In addition, the story included the umpteenth comparison to another quarterback, fellow Great Falls native Dave Dickenson. Dave preceded me at C.M. Russell High by three years. Besides being a tremendous player who would go on to star at Montana and in the Canadian Football League, he was also fairly perfect – polite, outgoing, respectful, a straight-A student. In other words, he was a lot of things I wasn't.

The article went so far as to say teachers in Great Falls would tell their students not to be like Ryan Leaf. It even included the joke: `What's the perfect football player? Dave Dickenson's head on Ryan Leaf's body.'

There must have been four or five quotes from different people about how I hated to lose. That was the bottom line on everything with me. It colored everything I did and everyone I knew. I don't think this was new ground being plowed. I had been called brash and confident in print many times, but the Montana angle on it all was new.

Except for the part about teachers warning their students about me, which seems a bit far-fetched, the story is pretty insightful. I think it upset my parents, especially Mom, because this was supposed to be a time of joy and celebration. In six days, the Cougars would be playing in the Rose Bowl for the first time in 67 years. Why spoil the ride with something so, well, not in keeping with the theme of the feel-good sports story of the year?

And I do mean feel good. From the moment we stopped UCLA at the goal line to win the season opener we were off to Pleasantville as far as media coverage was concerned. It started locally and regionally but soon USA Today, Sports Illustrated, The Sporting News and others were taking notice of us. Sports Illustrated spent a week in Pullman and published an incredible story on Jason McEndoo and Ryan McShane. Later in the season, SI gave us more of a back-handed compliment than an atta boy, calling us a "motley band of renegades and rejects." Coach Price was really miffed, and rightly so. While the way he built the team was somewhat unconventional, we were no band of thugs and clowns. Of the 26 seniors on the team, I believe every single one graduated. Still, the old saying that 'any publicity is good publicity', held for me because we're talking about Sports Illustrated. Sports Illustrated! Growing up that was like my Bible.

Mike Sando, now at ESPN.com, was the Spokesman-Review's Cougar beat writer at the time. He was just a youngster really, and must have felt like he'd won the lottery with this team. Besides winning at an unprecedented rate with a high-scoring offense, we were a team full of characters. Leon Bender and Chris Jackson were as quotable as they come. Five one-time walks-ons – five – were in the starting line-up: Cory Withrow, Lee Harrison, Shawn Tims, Todd Nelson and Rian Lindell. Mike Sage, a giant lineman with a giant appetite, could polish off 75 hot wings in one sitting. Starting defensive tackle Gary Holmes was the son of an Army drill sergeant whose brother moved in with the family when Gary was young and immediately put him on a fitness and training program. The list went on.

The headlines on Sando's stories seemed to jump off the sports page in jumbo-sized type with huge color photos accompanying them. "Darlings of Destiny Win in OT" . . . "Eyeing the Prize" . . . "A Nose for the Rose" . . . "Hats Off to the Cagey Leaf."

Mike and I got along well and we still talk every once in a while. He loves to jab me about the time in 1996 I threw a pass at his head during practice as retribution for a story of his I didn't like. I honestly don't recall doing it, but Mike has talked about it so long that it is now part of Cougar lore.

While he was the young gun at the Spokesman-Review, John Blanchette was the paper's seasoned columnist. He was someone you looked forward to reading, be it good or bad for your side. He had talent and humor coming out his ears. The funny phrases and metaphors he'd come up with often had me re-reading sentences to make sure I got 'em right. I always liked John, even though when it came to the Cougs, my sense was that in his eyes we were basically guilty until proven innocent. I remember he called me grumpy after we put 67 points on the board against Cal because I said I wasn't going to savor a rout. He was probably right. The Monday after we beat the Huskies he came out with a column asking if we were America's Team. John Blanchette was turning into a believer! That right there tells you how special our '97 team was.

My relationship with all the people who covered us was very good. Dale Grummert of the Lewiston Tribune was like Blanchette, with his clever and quirky style, and just a fun guy to talk with. Dick Rockne of the Seattle Times was like a sportswriter out of the movies. He had gray hair and a deep voice and asked questions so matter-of-factly. He was like the consummate professional. There were others, plus the TV guys from the Spokane stations, who were all good to work with, too. We obviously weren't in a big media market but the coverage of us was comprehensive and once we really got rolling the Seattle media started to amp it up.

I had a tendency to stick my foot in my mouth about how we were going to do this or do that and that got me in trouble from time to time, but never in any major way and never in a way that created animosity with the people who covered us. That might sound surprising to anyone who watched me flail so badly in the public eye in San Diego but it's true. Of course, when it came to the '97 season, there wasn't a whole lot of adversity to deal with so my temperament couldn't have gotten too out of whack.

Rod Commons, the long-time WSU Sports Information Director, was a true Godsend for me. He held my hand with everything when it came to dealing with the media. He protected me from myself more times than I can remember. Rod knew I hated to do sit-down interviews. Sit downs were so focused, so personal, I felt like I was in the middle of the crosshairs and had no convenient way to get out. These interviews required a little small talk, a little introspection and a lot of personality. I just felt out of place. Standing on the field after practice and answering questions, or talking on the phone, always seemed so much safer. I would complain about the sit downs but Rod would painstakingly tell me why it was important and make sure I was prepared.

For him, this was old hat. Rod had arrived at WSU in the 1970s, before Jack Thompson became the 'Throwin' Samoan' and started shattering national passing records. Between Jack, Mark Rypien, Timm Rosenbach and Drew Bledsoe, Rod had about as much experience handling the hoopla around celebrated quarterbacks as anyone in the nation. There wasn't a question he hadn't heard or anticipated. The one thing that may have thrown him for a loop was me. Jack, Mark, Timm and Drew do doubt were far better behaved and polished in their day than I was in mine.

That day I was rummaging through the boxes in my parents' basement I also found a bunch of videotapes of interviews I'd done at WSU. I'd never seen them before so I plugged a few into the machine. Embarrassing is about the only word to describe what I saw. I sounded just a little too confident for my britches, and I looked about 12 years old, which made it even worse.

RAIN DOWN ON ME
Apple Cup: 1997 Game 11

Dorian Boose summed it up pretty well heading into the Apple Cup, "A loss would be devastating. A win would be glorious – rays of sunshine, flowers blooming." While straight to the point, those weren't the quotes that made the headlines. In Sunday evening interviews the day after we beat Stanford, Chris Jackson had all but called the Huskies a bunch of dirty rotten scoundrels and predicted we'd light up the scoreboard on 'em for 40 or 50. The heat was already turned up on the 1997 Apple Cup because for the first time since 1981 the Cougars entered the big game with a trip to Pasadena on the line. Now it was getting turned up even more.

We were 9-1 and ranked 11th. The Huskies were 7-3 and ranked 16th. They had lost two-in-a row coming in, torpedoing season-long hopes for an Apple Cup with roses at stake for both sides. All was not lost for the Dawgs, however. As I recall, there was talk of them earning an invitation to the Cotton Bowl if they beat us. Despite our record, and the Huskies' losing skid, odds

215

makers opened betting with the Dawgs as six-and-a-half-point favorites. Yep, the game was in Seattle alright, but a touchdown favorite? After ten weeks of inspired football we were still fighting for respect.

To this day, Apple Cup week is my favorite time of the year because it unites so many people in so many ways. As a player, there is nothing more important than beating the arch-rival. You have to be careful, though, not to get too worked up because that's when you can make costly mistakes on the field. To the degree he could, Coach Price encouraged us to go about the week like any other.

CJ's harsh words made his job tougher. "I'll be damned if I'm going to let the Huskies get in my way of going to the Rose Bowl," CJ said. He called them cocky and overrated and said he didn't have "an ounce of respect for them." Fans, players, and reporters all seemed to be in the mood for a brawl – especially Coach Price. But the object of Mike's scorn wasn't the Dawgs, it was Chris.

Mike had made it very clear to us on Sunday that we were not to give 'em any bulletin board material, and then CJ went right out of the gate with guns blazing. He called me late that night with the bad news: Coach Price wanted to see him in the office at 6 a.m. "Ya gotta live with the consequences," I told Chris. There was no way to put the words back in the bottle. I wasn't in the room when he was being interviewed, so I didn't know until the next morning's newspaper exactly what was said. Oh man, I thought I sometimes stepped in it. This was a whole new level. Chris was always a good talker, but not a bomb thrower. It was out of character, and perhaps a statement of how much we wanted the win and how much we disliked the Dawgs. Chris' punishment came in two parts. First, he had to apologize to the Huskies. And second, he had to run. And run. And run some more. That 6 a.m. meeting was less about talking than it was about cardiovascular homicide. I don't recall how long CJ ran that morning, but I think the order was until he puked or fell over or both.

While Coach Price was stewing over it – I think he came close to breaking his hand pounding it on his desk – the rest of the team was hell-yeah-right-on with CJ. We all thought the same things he did, just not out loud in front of a reporter. We knew we had the firepower to back it up so we really couldn't have cared less what the Huskies put on their bulletin board. One of my favorite quotes of the week came from Dorian, in response to all the fallout about CJ. Being a Tacoma guy, he knew and liked a number of Husky players. It was the broader arrogance of the program that he didn't appreciate. "I'm mad at the Huskies as a concept," he said.

As much as I agreed with CJ's sentiments, I could sympathize with Coach Price. I can't imagine the pressure he felt that week, knowing that his own lifelong dream, and the dreams of two or three generations of Cougar fans, were riding on his every move. From Pullman to Spokane, Wenatchee to Yakima, Eastern Washington was buzzing about the Cougars. And so was Western Washington, with something like 60,000 alums living in the I-5 corridor. We truly were topic No. 1 across the state.

For the players, we couldn't get caught up in all the hoopla and hype. We had to, as Jim Walden might say, "dance with who brung ya to the ball." In our case, that meant focusing only on the job at hand. I didn't really feel like there was extra pressure going into this game. I felt like we had the best team in the country. The only way we could lose was by beating ourselves with unforced errors.

This is how comfortable I was with where we were standing. On Thursday after practice, less than 48 hours until kickoff, I was home having a beer and playing dominos with Dave Muir's brother Mike when the phone rang. Remember now, this is an era before widespread use of cell phones or the internet. You had to be home on a hard line in order to talk with someone. I answered and heard what sounded like a low-key party going on in the background, followed by a young woman's voice

"Is this Ryan?"

"Yep."

"My friends and I just saw your picture in the paper here at The Coug, and we thought, *you know what, we should buy that guy a beer.*"

"Seriously?"

'Heck, why not,' I thought. I consulted quickly with Mike, who expressed skepticism. "What's the downside?" I asked. "At worst, we get a free beer." He relented, and we head to The Coug. The girls were funny, and good looking, too, and we chatted and polished off a pitcher or two. It was the epitome of how quirky a college town can be. I didn't think about the Apple Cup at all that night. I relaxed. I enjoyed what college was about. It was so informal. I was being a normal student who happened to be the quarterback of a very good football team – and my phone number was in the directory like everyone else's. Could you imagine something like that happening in Seattle or Los Angeles?

That kind of break from the spotlight became more and more

important to me as the wins piled up in 1997. All of us on the team loved the attention we were getting, and I soaked it up because I felt like the hyper-competitiveness that put me in a bad light for so long, was now being validated. But the newfound celebrity meant that time, already consumed by school, practice, film study and games, was getting squeezed even more by increased interview requests and people just wanting to come up and say hello. It was definitely a thrill, but it also had me searching for quiet time.

I found it in a barber shop. Well, not just a barber shop, but The Barber Shop on Main Street in downtown Pullman. Every two weeks or so – usually the Thursday before a home game – I'd head down to see Dave Cuellar, the owner and operator. He would buzz my head short on the sides and leave about an inch on the top. The atmosphere was so relaxing. This was like a barber shop you see on TV, a friendly place to shoot the breeze. Dave was low key and everyone who walked into the place was low key. We'd talk mostly about cars, girls and football. Dave would talk about whatever you wanted to talk about, which I think usually meant I talked about myself a lot. I'd been going to Dave for a couple years, but this season the visits weren't about hair, they were a break from the building whirlwind around me. I didn't know it at the time, but Drew Bledsoe, Timm Rosenbach and John Olerud also used to get their hair cut by Dave when they were at WSU. It's probably not a huge coincidence, since Pullman isn't exactly loaded with barber shops, but I have to think those 30 minutes in Dave's chair were a nice break from the pressures they were feeling, too. The thing about Dave is that he treated everyone the same. The fact I was the Cougars' quarterback didn't impress him at all. To him, I was just

Ryan the loyal customer. That was probably another reason why I looked forward to getting my hair cut. It was just easy to be there.

§

Normally for a game in Seattle, Coach Price would put us on a bus first thing Friday morning, have a walkthrough practice at Husky Stadium, and then have our weekly meetings that night. This time, he decided to do something different. He didn't want us to be in Seattle that long. So we did our walkthrough practice at Martin Stadium on Friday afternoon, took a charter flight to Seattle, and then headed to the hotel for meetings, film, farewell speeches by the seniors and then bed. In short, he made the day more like the routine for a home game than a road game. Subconsciously I think that put everyone in a good place mentally. We also didn't stay downtown. Our hotel was in Lynnwood. Coach Price really didn't want any vibes at all from earlier trips to Seattle that had ended with the wrong team winning.

Farewell speeches by the seniors were a night-before-the-Apple Cup tradition at WSU. It's usually pretty nostalgic. This one started out that way, too. I had spent hours editing a highlight reel of all the seniors, put to music, and presented it to them as my thanks for being great teammates. As guys got up to speak, the mood started shifting from touching to hilarious. It basically turned into a variety show. CJ got up and started doing an impersonation of Coach Price that I think the guys are still talking about. This was the personality of the 1997 Cougars. The biggest game in school history, pretty much, is the next day and we're so relaxed we turn the farewell tour into a Saturday Night Live episode.

There was another surprise going into the Apple Cup besides this impromptu comedy night. Coach Price's older brother Geoff had flown in for the game, unannounced, from his home in Fresno. This was like something straight out of a script, because were it not for Geoff you'd have to think none of us would have become a Cougar. If he hadn't decided to go play ball for WSU in the 1950s, when Mike was still a kid, then Mike never would have become as devout a Cougar as he is. His whole life began to point to this very moment – an Apple Cup for the Rose Bowl – the day Geoff stepped onto Rogers Field.

§

Kickoff was at 12:30 so we were all up early. The Michigan-Ohio State game was on TV as we were getting taped and suited up. Charles Woodson returned a punt for a touchdown and made an interception. The Wolverines won 20-14, securing the Big Ten championship and finishing the regular season at 11-0. They had also locked down their No. 1 national ranking headed into the bowl season. "Look, we win this ball game, we're playing the No. 1 team in the country for the national championship," I announced to anyone within earshot. I didn't get much response, and that actually made perfect sense – these guys were workmen and they couldn't be bothered by distractions.

Our uniforms that day would be white jerseys and gray pants. We hadn't worn that combination the entire season, or even in my WSU career I don't believe. It had been decided upon by senior players who were part of the "advisory board" that Coach Price had in place to deal with different issues. I'm not sure why they wanted this combo – just something a little different for the rivalry game, I guess – but I was likin' it. Small stuff like that always gave me a charge. I remembered seeing highlight films of Mark Rypien wearing white and gray in 1985 – the last time WSU won in Husky Stadium. I thought it looked rockin', and having the advisory board put us in the same combination was a good omen. I was so excited by the idea that I asked our equipment manager, Josh Pietz, if he could get me a pair of white cleats. That would make a head-to-toe clean look – just like Kurt Russell in the old movie *The Best of Times*. With the team trailing, quarterback Reno Hightower (Russell) comes out from halftime – dramatic music playing – wearing white cleats. "Whoa Nellie, he's wearing his white shoes . . . the crowd's going wild," the press box announcer says. Yes, it sounds silly now, but for a 21-year-old kid there are big ways and small ones to produce your best, most competitive self on game day. And wearing white shoes for the first time in my Cougar career put a spring in my step.

Husky Stadium was a sellout. Actually, it was more than sellout, because they installed temporary stands in the northeast corner. They looked rickety but no one cared. We knew Husky Stadium would be hostile, but we also knew what this game meant to the Cougar Nation. They would figure out a way to get into this game, above and beyond the few thousand seats set aside in the west end zone. Looking up just before kickoff, I saw flashes of crimson all over the place – two people here, four people there. This was a road game, yes, but we had a small Cougar army with us in there. Every pass we completed, every run our defense snuffed would be greeted with cheers. Glenn Johnson, the amazing Cougar P.A. announcer – and also my adviser in the Murrow School – was obviously not working a road game, but he and his son were in the stands that day. Every time we did something good, you could almost hear your mind channeling the best of Glenn: "And that's another . . . Cougar first down!"

The weather was overcast with a chance of rain. Rain always bothered me. I couldn't grip the ball the way I wanted. It was in my head a little bit, but it never affected me against the Huskies thanks to Mike Price. Once a week that entire season he'd bring out a bucket of water and make me dunk my hand, and the ball, in it before every throw in skeleton or one-on-one drills. I was absolutely defiant against this. I called it "destroy Ryan's self-esteem day" because I became inaccurate, unable to throw consistently, or even put a decent spiral on the ball. My defiance turned this exercise into a mandatory part of every week.

So here we are four months later, playing our first game in rain. And I was completely oblivious to it. To this day, if someone asked me if it rained at the 1997 Apple Cup I'd have to say I only know that it did from watching replays. I had thrown so many wet balls over the course of the season that it was now like muscle memory. Been there, done that. This was another example of Coach Price turning a weakness into a strength. It was also a prime example of how small things that fans never see can make all the difference in a game's outcome.

One thing Coach Price couldn't coach around was my swollen right thumb. On the third play of the game, I made a throw down the left side of the field, and as I released it, my thumb got caught in Husky linebacker Jason Chorak's helmet and ended up getting twisted and pulled before the play was done. It was dislocated and sprained and started to swell like a balloon. As I came off the field, I put my hand in my waist pouch and hid it behind my back so Coach Price couldn't see it as we talked about the next series. When we finished, I walked over to Mark Smaha and he started to do his thing. He fixed the dislocation, informed me it was just sprained, and that there was nothing else to be done if I wanted to throw a football the rest of the day. I never once let Coach Price see my thumb. Every time I came off the field I had my hand in the pouch behind my back. The thumb bothered me, for sure, but I was still able to grip the ball.

While Mark was working on me, the game was getting off to a bad start. The Huskies drove 71 yards on their first possession and led 7-0. Our defense tightened up after that, but on offense we were struggling – until Love Jefferson lit a fire. He was a junior tight end who had come to WSU when the University of the Pacific folded its program. We hooked up for a quick pass over the middle late in the first quarter and was tackled by his facemask. Penalty flags flew. Going down by the facemask is one very dangerous proposition, and Love erupted out of the pile. He threw the ball down and said "come on we're right here," effectively telling the Huskies that if they wanted to play rough we'd much rather go toe-to-toe than engage in that kind of cheap stuff. It was like a switch being turned on. Football is a physical game, but it's also an emotional one, especially at the college level, and actions like Love's can sometimes prove as invaluable as a great block, catch , run or tackle.

224

We proceeded to score 17 unanswered points, including a TD that would become one of the most iconic in WSU and Apple Cup history. We were on our own 43, facing a third-and-12. At the line of scrimmage, they were playing safety high (i.e. in the middle of the field) with the corner on the left side pressing Chris Jackson. In film studies that week, their corners looked to be on the smaller side and they tended to trail in coverage, meaning fade routes could be highly effective. My mouth almost started watering when I saw how they were set up on this one. I looked over at CJ, and checked into what we called our 63 package. I took a five-step drop, looked briefly to the right to hold the safety, and then turned left and let the ball go high over CJ's outside shoulder.

It ended up being a perfect pass, because CJ kept the defender on his inside shoulder. No one was going to catch that ball but CJ It worked exactly as we practiced it. CJ stopped for a split-second after catching the ball to let the corner fly past him. The safety, Tony Parrish, had a lot of ground to cover but was coming in hard. CJ ducked his shoulder at the moment of impact, hitting Parrish in the head and sending him to the ground. Parrish grabbed an ankle, but CJ wriggled out and covered the final 15 yards with the crowd going nuts. In all, it was a 57-yard scoring strike that put us up 14-7. Our sideline went crazy. That play signified what the season was about, what we were about. We had prepared for what we saw on film, we executed it, and then we made that extra special play to turn it into six points. That was the turning point in the ballgame. From that point on, I didn't feel there was anything Washington could do to stop us.

The tone was really set on the Huskies' next series. Brock Huard threw a misdirection screen pass to Cam Cleland, their outstanding tight end, and it was set up perfectly. He had nothing but green and a team of blockers ahead of him. Almost out of nowhere, our leading tackler, sophomore linebacker Steve Gleason, entered the picture. I say "out of nowhere" because Steve was easy to miss in a game full of 6-5, 300-pounders. He was 5-11 and listed at 215 but was more like 205. He was one tough little hombre and this play proved it. He and Cleland collided so hard it's no exaggeration to say they heard the impact in the upper deck. Cleland, who weighed 275, was lifted a foot off the ground. He managed to stay on his feet long enough to gain an extra yard. Steve, meanwhile, was down on the turf with a shoulder stinger. He got up pretty quickly and came over to the sideline, thinking Cleland had gotten the best of him. But Cleland was still lying on the turf. "He's not getting up!" someone shouted. It sent a shiver through our sideline. Steve gave up 70 pounds on that exchange and we still won. That's called 'a football play' right there. This was more evidence, in our minds, that we were not going to be denied our place in Pasadena. Steve, by the way, was back in the lineup on the very next play. Cleland wasn't. Ironically, the two of them would later become teammates on the New Orleans Saints.

On offense we were converting every long third-down play and I felt like I couldn't miss a throw if I tried. Chorak, their linebacker, was Mr. Blitz and came close to sacking me a couple of times, but the Fat Five made sure he never quite got there, so I started jawing at him. "Nice try there four-six" . . . "Good effort four-six" . . . "Keep trying four-six" . . . "Maybe next time four-six." He was no shrinking violet so we had this "conversation" going on most of the game. I have to smile about it to this day because I knew I was annoying the hell out of him.

We were the most prolific offense in Pac-10 history and No. 2 in the country that season, and we were showing the reasons why in the second quarter. And our defense, after giving up that first-possession TD to the Dawgs, went on a pick-off spree. Every time Brock Huard went deep, one of our defensive backs was there to intercept. Dee Moronkola nabbed the first one, Ray Jackson the second, and Lamont Thompson the third. Huard would throw two more picks in the second half – both taken by Lamont. Those five picks for the day by Huard equaled his total from the entire rest of the season. I always thought that stat was a fine tribute to our defensive coordinator, Bill Doba, and our defense. For Lamont, who was just a true freshman, it was a coming out party that foreshadowed his eventual place among the all-time greats at WSU. Besides the air thefts, he had a team-high 12 tackles against the Huskies. He was in the lineup in place of injured senior Duane Stewart, who was a very talented player. The fact we could replace Duane with a kid like Lamont spoke to the depth we had on this team.

We went into halftime with a 17-7 lead and then extended it to 24-7 when Rob Rainville – yes, left tackle Rob Rainville – scored about five minutes into the third quarter. After Huard's fourth interception, we drove down to the two-yard-line. Michael Black, who ran wild for us all day and scored our first TD, lost the handle on this one and Rob recovered in the end zone. Scoring the TD was great but having the big guy from Lewiston get the glory was just over the top. Fate, it seemed, truly was on our side.

Or maybe not. The Huskies proceeded to score 14 points in

the span of three minutes – once on a four-play drive set up by a long kickoff return and then on an interception Tony Parrish took back 32 yards. On the interception, we were down around our own one and I thought I could pull off a play that would suck the wind out of the Dawgs. It was a pass across the middle that had worked a couple times earlier in the game. This time, however, I forgot to look off the safety and Parrish made me pay dearly. The stadium was shaking. The PAT narrowed the score to 24-21 and now the home crowd was salivating. Everyone tried to tell me it was all right when I got to the sideline, but I was ready to slap myself. Coach Price and I talked about what I did wrong, and then started brainstorming what we wanted to do when we went back out. On the fifth play of that series, I saw something I'd seen before – something I liked – in the Husky defense. I audibled the same play Chris Jackson and I had connected on earlier for the big TD, only this time we were going to do it on the right side of the field. Fifty yards later, we were up 31-21.

This was the Apple Cup. As the '95 and '96 games had illustrated, it's never over until it's over We traded blows in the fourth quarter and then the Dawgs scored on a long TD pass from Huard to Jerome Pathon with nine seconds left. That brought the score to 41-35, and they had time for an onside kick and a Hail Mary to win it. I was angry – not because they scored but because someone started passing roses around our bench about a minute before that scoring play. This is the Apple Cup. Nothing is decided. Those roses are going to jinx this.

My heart was pounding as they lined up for the onside kick. The ball dribbled straight ahead and there, like a guardian angel, was No. 45 – Shawn McWashington – to pounce on it. Even then, I wasn't ready to relax. All I had to do was go out and take a knee but for me nothing was certain until the clock read zero. In the huddle, the ever-funny Chopper (Ryan McShane) piped in. "So what do we have – a pass play?" I was still so focused, so aware there was time left that I not only failed to laugh but gave him a glare and a few choice words. As the Fat Five turned around to head to the line of scrimmage for the final snap, I thought how proud I was to be their quarterback, to have McShane, Rainville, Jason McEndoo, Cory Withrow and Lee Harrison in front of me on this journey of a lifetime.

I took the snap from Lee, went to a knee, and it was over. For the first time in 67 years, Washington State was going to the Rose Bowl. As our sideline emptied, I took off toward the end zone, where so many of our fans were sitting, to spike the ball (stupid, I know, because I have no idea what happened to it). Cougar fans were pouring onto the field. As I ran back toward my teammates, somebody handed me a hat and a rose, and then all of a sudden I was in the air, hoisted up by this mass of crimson humanity that seemed to materialize on the field almost instantly. The entire field was covered – as were the goalposts – in Cougars celebrating a championship for the first time since 1930. "The rain must have been the tears of Babe Hollingbery and Mel Hein," Shawn McWashington would tell reporters.

Amid the craziness, I heard the Husky P.A. announcer say "Congratulations to Washington State and best of luck in Pasadena." That was such a classy thing to say. Some of the Husky players stayed on the field for a while and watched. I don't blame them. Whether you won or lost, wore crimson or purple, this was a spectacle.

When I did my post-game interview with ABC, I was just out of breath. I was searching for words that I just couldn't come up with. *What had we just done? What did this mean? What were we gonna do now?*

The locker room was bedlam. This wasn't just a year's worth of hard work coming to fruition. For the redshirt seniors it was five years of striving. I looked down at my thumb, which Coach Price still wouldn't learn about until the next day, and it seemed like it was about the size of my head. I was soaking wet, too. I had just thrown for 358 yards – in the rain – with a bad thumb. I couldn't have done that in '96. The extra year of maturity, the extra year of team building, the extra year of tutoring from Mike Price all added up to this day. We were destined to do this. The site of my first start as quarterback of the Cougs – on a day two years earlier that was filled with hope but ultimately a loss – was now the site of my last conference game as a Cougar. This time it wasn't a feeling of hope, but one of accomplishment for having turned hope into the ultimate prize: playing in the Rose Bowl against the No. 1 team in the nation.

As an athlete, this was the greatest day of my life, made more special because my family was there to share in it. I knew first-hand how jubilant they were along with my teammates and coaches. Still I wouldn't truly understand how it affected Cougar fans until I was in my 30s and started reconnecting with them after the self-imposed exile that followed my disappointing pro career. We had captured their imaginations in a way that transcended our sport.

We brought people together, uniting a community, and showing the entire nation what we already knew: Washington State isn't just a school, but a culture that stays with you for life.

The celebration on the field hinted at the lasting impact – it went on forever. The giant crimson leaf flag that the cheer squad had been toting around the field during the game got torn to shreds, and my mom, dad, aunt and uncle got little pieces of it. I was born to be a college quarterback. I was born to be a Cougar. And on that day in Seattle I felt I was born to help make history.

The front page of the Spokesman-Review the next day summed it up well. Under the banner headline "A Wazzu Bouquet" was a color picture of Mike and Joyce Price hugging next to a huge display of roses. The story it accompanied started off this way: "It was better than Christmas, more festive than New Year's, bigger than all the holidays put together. Like a long-awaited homecoming, Washington State University's triumph over arch rival Washington sent Cougar fans into a frenzy."

GOING DOWNTOWN

My mom, Marcia, is about the nicest person in the world. Nurses are caring people by nature and she fits that description to a tee. In nearly 40 years as a parent, stretching from me to my brothers Jeffrey and Brady, she has never stopped worrying about us and taking care of us. So when the call came from New York inviting me to the Heisman Trophy presentation, Mom was concerned because her son had nothing to wear.

Walking into the Downtown Athletic Club in blue jeans and a sweatshirt wasn't going to work. Walking in wearing a polyester suit wasn't going to do, either. This was the big time and Mom knew it. Unbeknownst to me, she had pored over the family budget with the goal of saving $1,000 that could be rerouted to dressing me up. When she hit her total, she called and told me to meet her in Spokane. She was driving in from Great Falls and headed straight downtown to Nordstrom's.

I don't know how it all was arranged, one of the folks at WSU I presume, but we walked into Nordstrom's one morning – I think it was before they actually opened for business – and were greeted by a personal shopper who was waiting for us and eager to assist. For me, this was downright nuts. Life was definitely changing in a big way.

Being oblivious to cost and fashion sense, I wanted to get whatever I wanted to get, but Mom had a strict budget and wasn't going to let a penny of it go to waste. So everything had to look sharp and fit perfectly. I walked out with a beautiful charcoal gray suit, French blue dress shirt and silk neck tie, plus a nice sport coat and slacks. For a guy who spent most of the previous four years in jeans, sweats and gym shorts, this was all quite a change. I have to say the blue shirt turned out to be killer, because the other three Heisman finalists – Tennessee's Peyton Manning, Michigan's Charles Woodson and Marshall's Randy Moss – were all wearing white shirts the night of the presentation. My tie really brought everything together though. It was red and blue and had falling leaves on it. Yes, it obviously fit my last name, but more importantly it was reminiscent of the Heisman campaign Coach Price had launched for me – mailing large maple leafs to voters across the country.

I always tell people I was a football fan long before I was a football player, so getting invited to the Heisman presentation was the thrill of a lifetime – one I wasn't going to miss a minute of. I brought a video camera with me to capture this unique piece of history. And it was unique, because Woodson was the first defensive player ever to win it. I knew I didn't have a chance to win, which meant I had no pressure on me at all. I was just there to have fun and to be a fan of the sport I love.

Before heading to New York for the big event, I had one stop to make – in Orlando for the Davey O'Brien Award, which goes to the top quarterback in the country, and the Maxwell Award, which is presented to the top college football player. I was booked on a red-eye flight out of Seattle to Atlanta, where I would then connect to Orlando. As fate would have it, a familiar face was in the gate area when I arrived – Husky All-American wide receiver Jerome Pathon. Two weeks earlier we would have just as soon spit on each other as talk, but outside the field of battle there's a mutual respect that comes from knowing the other guy spent as much blood, sweat and tears for his side as you did for yours. We started talking and decided we ought to sit together on the plane. We soon decided to toast the glory of Cougars and Huskies with those miniature liquor bottles they serve on planes. Coupled with my aforementioned video camera, this proved to be a nicely documented case of why the 21-year-old drinking age might be a tad on the young side.

I spent the next two days in Orlando, with my dad joining me. At the awards show I met some of the greatest college football players in the country, from Daunte Culpepper to Ricky Williams. I was star struck. I had my video camera running damn near the whole time. I was still a guy that watched these people play on TV and was in awe of them, yet here I was as a peer. The show itself was amazing. Coach Price was there and won the National Coach of the Year Award. I was so proud to see him on stage, recognized as the best in the entire country. Peyton won both the O'Brien and the Maxwell awards. I was skunked but still considered myself a winner, because I was there representing Washington State on the national stage.

From there it was on to New York, where my mom, brother Brady, aunt Caroline and uncle Charlie would join me and my dad. The Downtown Athletic Club, located in Lower Manhattan, was something to behold – a brick skyscraper that had been around since the 1930s and hosted the Heisman presentation ever since. This was history I was walking into – the same building where Roger Staubach, Jim Plunkett, Bo Jackson, Barry Sanders and so many other legends had walked. Little did anyone know at the time, but we would be one of the final groups of Heisman finalists to be celebrated in this historic place. The club went bankrupt and shut down after the attacks on 9/11. It wasn't because of structural damage, but because it was a few blocks from ground zero and became part of the "frozen zone" during the clean up. There was no way for the club to financially stay afloat that long without any business.

One of my clearest images from the Heisman ceremony was Chris Fowler stepping up to the podium before the broadcast began and saying, "If you're in this room, you either know somebody or are somebody." The moment he said that I wanted to turn around and smile at my mom and dad. I went into this event knowing that I wasn't going to win. From a regional perspective, I figured Peyton had the south and southwest, Charles the midwest and maybe the east. As it turned out, I was second to Woodson in the only region I thought I had a shot at taking: the far west. I truly presumed Peyton Manning was going to win in a walk, with Charles coming in second. I was just happy to be there. I was part of this. I was a Heisman finalist. I was with these great players, and I was being honored for what our incredible players and coaches had been able to do at WSU. As a kid, you dream about something like this.

At a function before the ceremony, all the finalists and their families and coaches got a chance to visit. My folks hit it off with the Mannings and have stayed friends all these years. Brady, my youngest brother, and Eli, Peyton's younger brother, were close to the same age. I have a picture of the two of them sitting next to each other. They were just kids and thrilled to be there. Years later, Brady would play quarterback for the Oregon Ducks and Eli of course would become a standout at Mississippi before leading the New York Giants to a Super Bowl victory.

The night was interesting. I did an interview with Kirk Herbstreit, and made a point to acknowledge every one of my teammates on the offensive side of the ball because truly, I felt that if I hadn't had them – if they weren't a part of who I was – there was no way I was going to be a Heisman Trophy candidate. Herbie was probably hoping I'd shut up, but I did in fact mention every single person on the offensive side of the ball that night.

When the moment came that they announced the winner, there wasn't really any nervous energy from me. I knew I was an afterthought, but I was really shocked when they announced Charles Woodson. He had turned in a tremendous season and was incredibly talented – as I would later learn firsthand in the Rose Bowl – but defensive players never won the Heisman. He was the first and, as of this point, still the only one ever to do it. I don't know if Peyton was as shocked as I was. If so, he hid it well. He was sitting on Charles' immediate left and was quick to extend a handshake. I remember seeing a photo of that moment – Randy Moss is sitting there in Oakley sunglasses like he's too cool to care.

Peyton looks very professional shaking Charles' hand, and I'm leaning over, getting ready to shake his hand. I always thought my posture and the look on my face really captured my outlook on the whole thing: I was relaxed and just enjoying the opportunity to be there.

Charles was a very charismatic guy, a guy with a huge personality but graced with the humility of being raised by an amazing woman. He was cocky for sure, but he certainly could back it up in everything he did. He was a well-deserving winner of the award and represented it with respect.

Shortly after the ceremony, Coach Price and I went to see a taping of Saturday Night Live at 30 Rockefeller Center. The hosts were Helen Hunt and Jack Nicholson. That alone would have made the trip to NYC memorable. But here I was in the land of football royalty. After the taping we went to a local bar where all the former Heisman winners, plus Herbstreit and Fowler, were schmoozing. I even took a turn bartending. It was so much fun. I felt like such a grownup. I felt like I had just accomplished so much, interacting with everybody, and then I looked over to see my father in the corner of the room standing with Tony Dorsett, Archie Griffin, all these past winners – all these greats that he admired and watched. And the smile on his face for those two or three hours into the late night just warmed my heart. That was what it was all about.

To top the night off, I met a lovely young woman who was the granddaughter of one of the winners from the 1950s. We spent the night drinking and talking and getting to know one another, and stayed in touch for a few years. We also learned something about the age of the Downtown Athletic Club. The rooms were heated by those extremely hot, ancient iron radiators. When her family decided to give her an early wake-up call the next morning, I rolled off the bed and leaned up against the radiator with my back. To say that it was scalding doesn't begin to describe the heat. If I didn't have incentive enough to get out of there, this definitely jump-started the process.

Other than this mild misfortune, the weekend was perfect. The Heisman experience lived up to every expectation and probably exceeded them. I remember as we left, Coach Price said in an interview, "I can't believe I'm saying this about Ryan, but he was just absolutely a class act and a gentleman." Given some of my history, that meant a lot to hear. As corny as it may sound, I felt like I had to raise my social game back there because I was representing Washington State. I also felt like I had a responsibility to carry the torch high for four great Cougars who finished in the top 10 in Heisman voting before me – Ed Goddard, Jack Thompson, Timm Rosenbach and Drew Bledsoe – but didn't get the chance to experience the ceremony and hoopla around the award. I was able to because I had the most talented supporting cast of any Cougar quarterback in history. That's opinion, of course, not fact. With all due respect to Lone Star Dietz, Mel Hein and Jason Gesser, I'll go to my grave knowing the 1997 Washington State Cougars were the greatest team ever to roam the Palouse.

A few weeks after New York, back home in Montana before leaving for the Rose Bowl, my family set up a celebration for me at a local brew pub. When I arrived, I found a banner that read "Ryan Leaf's Montana Heisman Presentation." I didn't quite understand what that meant. But as I walked in my family and placed me in a chair and announced that I was the recipient of the Montana Heisman. I was surrounded by family, friends and former teammates from high school, so I had a hunch something interesting was about to unfold. Sure enough, they brought out a mounted white tail deer in a beautiful trophy case. This was no ordinary white tail either. It was one I'd shot years before. I was so touched by this and all the folks who'd come out for it. That night it really hit me how powerful sports can be in uniting and uplifting a community. Pullman and the Cougar Nation naturally had come together in an unprecedented way but now here was my hometown getting fired up because one of their own had succeeded on a national scale.

The biggest honor I would receive that season was still to come, however. A few nights into our stay in Santa Monica while preparing for the Rose Bowl, a bunch of us wandered over to a little bar called "Chillers." In the corner there was a Miller Lite display with a cardboard cutout of the Heisman Trophy. I didn't notice it, but before the night was over, Cory Withrow, our right guard, had disassembled the display and taken the Heisman cutout. Before I knew it, he was standing on the bar speaking, with Ryan McShane, our right tackle, and Jason McEndoo, our left guard, soon to join him.

"This is what really counts," said Cory. "This is what it's really all about, Ryan. You are our Heisman winner and we want to award this to you." He held out this giant cardboard cutout, and I walked up and gave a silly acceptance speech. Now while this was going on the manager of the establishment was getting antsy for the 900 pounds of offensive linemen to get off the bar. I concluded my speech by starting to sing the Cougar fight song and within seconds the whole place is singing it. We're all clapping, and as we finish we are very rudely removed from the premises.

I carried that trophy with me the rest of the night, to every bar we stopped in, and I still have it to this day. Coming from our offensive line – some of the hardest-working people I've ever been around – this public display of affection, presented as only 21- and 22-year-old college students can, really meant a lot to me.

THAT IS NO MISPRINT

At virtually every Cougar football game played in Pullman, you can count on about half of the entire student body to be in the stands. That is a tradition of support I'm hard-pressed to think any school in the nation could even come close to matching. So it shouldn't have been surprising that they'd be out in force the day Rose Bowl tickets went on sale. But I was stunned. They were lined up for hours outside Beasley Coliseum, on a cold, rainy day, and the line seemed like it wrapped all the way to Moscow. Hearing about something like that is one thing but to actually see it is quite another.

I was just blown away – so blown away that I did something very uncharacteristic, given my tendency to be selfish and strapped for cash. I went down to Dissmore's and bought four or five boxes of donuts to bring up to these spirited kids who make WSU the unique school it is. Of course, I was probably a good 800 boxes short of demand, but I felt like I needed to do something to say

241

thanks. As I walked through the line thanking everyone I told them the cold they were feeling today would melt away when we were all gathered in Pasadena on January 1.

It turns out the long line of students at Beasley was just the tip of what Rose Bowl officials said was the heaviest demand for tickets in two decades. WSU received 350,000 requests for tickets. That is no misprint – 350,000. The Rose Bowl, at that time, seated over 100,000. WSU, all by itself, could have filled three-and-a-half Rose Bowls. Of all the statistics and articles and interviews that help characterize a season, that one number all by itself – 350,000 – captures the excitement and mania that made the 1997 Cougars so memorable. We weren't undefeated and we didn't win the national championship, but we were a living, breathing example of the American ideal: If you work hard enough, long enough – and catch a break or two along the way – you're going to make it.

While the massive ticket demand spoke volumes about us – and about No. 1 Michigan – the sad reality is that it meant a lot of people weren't going to be able to go to the game. WSU was given 35,000 seats to sell and Michigan was given 26,000. The Rose Bowl handled the other 41,000. Based on the colors in the stands when game day arrived, I think the Cougar faithful put their hands on the majority of those 41,000. The face value of tickets was $75, but scalpers reportedly were getting up to $900 for them. One person who had no idea of the magnitude of it all was my mom. She compiled a list of every aunt, uncle, cousin and special friend who wanted to go to the game and then called the WSU ticket office and said, "Hello, this is Marcia Leaf. I'm Ryan's mom. I'd like 76 tickets to the Rose Bowl please." I think the woman who answered must have worked hard not to laugh, but politely responded that she could get Mom four seats. Mom might be a little embarrassed by that story but get this: Somehow, some way, she rounded up 76 tickets by the time the plane left Great Falls for Los Angeles.

Each player was allotted exactly two complimentary tickets. Mom didn't ask me to contribute mine to her collection. She felt I'd earned them and needed to decide for myself who they should go to, though I did consult with her and Dad before making the final call. I gave them to my high school coach, Jack Johnson, and his wife Roseanne. Coach Johnson didn't want me to go to WSU and our relationship deteriorated after I verbally committed to the Cougs. My decision to give him the tickets was made part out of appreciation, because I truly looked up to him when I was in high school, and part out of pride, because there was no greater validation of my college choice than playing in the Granddaddy of the Them All on New Year's Day.

The "Great Ticket Chase" wasn't the only post-Apple Cup surprise awaiting me. After the Husky game, I went home for Thanksgiving break and got a call Monday from Rod Commons, Sports Information Director at WSU. ESPN Game Day wanted to talk with me and Charles Woodson, together, live, on Thanksgiving Day. Three days later, this giant satellite truck pulls onto 29th Avenue Northeast in Great Falls and in less than an hour my parents' living room was turned into a TV studio. In the meantime, my mom was getting dinner ready for all the family that was coming over. This was just surreal. It was like I had been transported into someone else's life. This was the kind of thing Danny Wuerffel or Troy Aikman did, not Ryan Leaf from Great Falls. People on our block were gathering around outside. I remember looking at my dad, who is pretty reserved, and thinking this was the farthest thing from his mind during all those early morning hours he'd play catch with me in the backyard before going to work. I don't remember a thing about the interview that day, but the sight of the satellite truck outside and all the cables running into the house is one I'll never forget.

Over the next few weeks I'd travel to Florida and New York for the various awards ceremonies, and the publicity just flowed. I was meeting famous people, staying at nice hotels, having fancy dinners and being interviewed by reporters from all over the country. I loved it at the time, but in retrospect it was fueling a problem. The higher and higher I seemed to be placed on a pedestal, the more arrogant, defensive, and entitled I became. Years later, watching interview tapes of myself from that window of time, I saw hints that I was devolving from the team-oriented guy I had been the entire season to someone focused inwardly.

Also aiding and abetting my self-absorption was the NFL speculation. Would I stay or would I go? Aside from the Rose Bowl hype and preparation, that seemed to be the question on many minds. While I had decided in November that I was going pro, I didn't share that with too many people outside my family and Coach Price. Media speculation was really cooking in the lead up to the Rose Bowl – How high would I go? Would I go ahead of Peyton Manning? – I didn't want an announcement of me leaving to overshadow the Rose Bowl, so I just kept quiet. The Leaf vs. Manning debate had actually started to gain traction around mid-season, so I had called Peyton then to tell him how impressed I was with the way he played and conducted himself and that I didn't want the media to put a bogus wedge between us. Not surprisingly, Peyton was as gracious and friendly as he comes across on TV. Later, when I really had to confront my NFL decision, I called Peyton to pick his brain because he had faced the same situation the season before. The draft would of course connect our two names forever, but we have stayed in touch – as have our parents – all these years later.

Peyton wasn't the only person whose insights I sought with regard to a decision about the NFL. Jack Thompson, who had been a mentor to me since the day I stepped on campus, was at this same crossroads in the late '70s. He chose to return for one more year and, in the process, cemented his stature as probably the greatest Cougar ever. What he has done off the field over the years has only reinforced that perception. Jack is basically the godfather of Cougar quarterbacks, having taken virtually all of us under his wing, offering advice and guidance on both football matters and life generally. During games, if things weren't going our way, he'd often come up and whisper a word of encouragement in my ear. When people talk about the family atmosphere of WSU, this is the kind of thing they're referring to – helping each other, staying loyal, covering your back. At the time, I'm not sure I appreciated how generous this was of Jack, but as I've gotten older I find myself frequently looking at him as the ultimate role model. As I pondered my future, to stay or go, Jack was naturally one of the people I talked with. Drew Bledsoe was another. He came at it from a different place than Jack, because he had left school early. Jake Plummer and Warren Moon were others I talked with. My parents and Coach

Price, of course, were the biggest sounding boards. Ultimately, once everyone had helped me compile the pros and cons, they all had the same advice: Only you can know in your heart what the right decision is.

The plain fact is that in my discussions with people I wasn't so much looking for an answer as some ground-breaking reason I hadn't thought of to stay put. I had dreamed of the NFL my entire life, and was in position to be drafted at or near the top of the first round. Unless someone came up with a silver bullet reason, I was going. I truly felt like I was born to play quarterback. To get a lucrative chance to play it as the highest level was impossible for me to pass up – a decision I would later regret, but a done deal at the time.

While I knew my choice before the Apple Cup, the outpouring of emotion across the Cougar Nation after that title-clinching win tugged at my heart – to the point I told Coach Price during the Heisman Trophy presentation that I was coming back to WSU. The fans' reaction to what we had done was overwhelming, and the response from former Cougar players brought tears to my eyes. Old teammates of Jack's and Drew's and others, who were older and younger and in between, told us how proud they were and how gratifying it was to see us accomplish what they had wanted to do when they were wearing the uniform. Our season at its pinnacle was built on their steps. They had helped create the uncommon spirit at WSU. They had fostered the culture that said you never stop trying, you never stop fighting. We were the ones winning the games but a little piece of every one of those guys, who put on a crimson jersey before we did, was out there on the field with us.

This wasn't just our team. This was the Cougar family's team.

We practiced for the Rose Bowl at the L.A. Coliseum and every day old Cougar ballplayers would come by to watch and say hello. The day before Christmas, a police car pulled through the tunnel and the officer got out and asked who was in charge. Coach Price walked over and the officer told him some Cougar players were in trouble. Mike fell for it. It turns out the police officer was Randal Simmons, a WSU defensive back from the late-1970s. Randal, whose son Matthew now plays for WSU, was a Los Angeles Police Department S.W.A.T team member who was killed in the line of duty in 2008. Mike Levenseller went to his funeral and said it was clear Randal held four things closest to his heart: his family, his church, his job, and being a Cougar. Randal's old WSU jersey was on display at the services. That's the depth of loyalty WSU inspires in its people. That's why our Rose Bowl berth transcended our one team and that one season.

"Generations of Cougar fans and players have waited for this chance," Keith Lincoln, one of the greatest stars ever at WSU, told the Seattle Times. "It's a game for the generations, for the whole school and for the last 60 years." As a player and later a coach and administrator at WSU, Keith had a front-row seat to decades of Cougar football. Through it all, he said, he never, ever, lost faith that WSU would one day get to the Rose Bowl.

§

Preparing for a game in a place other than Pullman was really odd. The routine was out the window. I wasn't in Coach Price's office watching film, waiting for Joyce Price to walk in with a pumpkin pie, which she did every Thursday night, or taking a break with Mike to watch The Drew Carey Show, which we did every Wednesday. I wasn't eating baby back ribs for dinner, which I did once a week with Sharika Higgins, a pal of mine from the Cougar track team, who inadvertently became part of one of my superstitions and patiently agreed to eat ribs with me for the rest of the season in order to stave off all kinds of bad luck for the team.

Instead, I was partaking in a Cougars vs. Wolverines steak-eating contest at Lawry's Restaurant. Or riding in a limo with Shawn McWashington to a Lakers game to represent WSU in a Rose Bowl promotion. Or helping charge up a giant crowd of Cougs at a pep rally on the Santa Monica Pier. The journey from Great Falls to Pullman to all this seemed unreal.

We had arrived in Los Angeles about 10 days before the game. Our hotel was in Santa Monica, close to the beach and lots of bars. That may sound like a recipe for distraction, but it really wasn't. Sure, we had fun – a ton of fun in fact, but Coach Price knew exactly what kind of team this was. We were loaded with upper-classmen, which meant we knew how to handle ourselves. And our team personality was fun loving. We would respond positively to a little freedom, negatively to big constraints. Going to the Rose Bowl was a reward for a great season, not a ticket to prison camp.

"I believe if you treat people like adults, they'll be adults. If you treat them like kids, they'll act like kids. Last night we had a bed check at midnight and everybody was in," Coach Price said. Our practices were focused, efficient, effective – and family and friends could watch. There wasn't much hitting, because we'd just come through a punishing season and Coach Price wanted us fresh and healthy.

Michigan took a dramatically different approach. Their practices were closed, reporters' access to them was minimal, and they had two-a-days for their first week in town. That may have been the best approach for that team's personality. Every group is different and every coach has his own style. Lloyd Carr of Michigan was a no-nonsense disciplinarian. Mike Price was an optimistic, gregarious tour-de-force. Each did what worked for his personality and his players. I was glad to be on Mike Price's side of the field.

PUMPKIN PIE AND VANISHING TIME
The 1998 Rose Bowl

The way I viewed it, we were playing for the national championship. Michigan was undefeated and No. 1 in the country in both the Associated Press and Coaches Poll, while we were 10-1 and the champions of the Pac-10. It was the nation's No. 1-rated defense vs. the No. 2-rated offense. It was the Heisman winner vs. the Heisman finalist. All – and I use that word loosely – we needed to do was defeat the Wolverines, and then hope for divine intervention that No. 2 Nebraska and No. 3 Tennessee could somehow defeat each other in the Orange Bowl.

In other words, we weren't really playing for the national title on the first day of 1998, because no matter how well we performed, being ranked No. 8 going into the game made it impossible to leapfrog the winner of the Cornhuskers and Volunteers game. Regardless, I can tell you right now that in a perfect world – a world where the final two seconds on the Rose Bowl clock are restored and the ensuing play becomes Flutie-esque in its outcome – I would have told anybody within earshot who the rightful national champions were.

The Wolverines were seven-and-a-half-point favorites against us, but as near as I could tell, everybody from Keith Jackson to Bob Griese saw this one shaping up as a thriller. That's exactly what they got, too. In fact, it was better than a thriller because it ended in controversy.

From my standpoint, we couldn't have been in better position going into this one. First, we were healthy. That was one of the keys to our entire year but in the last few weeks of the season our secondary started to get dinged up. Those guys – Duane Stewart, Dee Moronkola, Ray Jackson, LeJuan Gibbons – had been unsung heroes all season. And then when injuries started to pop up, Lamont Thompson and Torry Hollimon had stepped up. Duane, our starting strong safety, actually had missed the last three games of the regular season with a knee injury. He was back for the Rose Bowl and would be counted on in a big way to help contain Michigan tight end Jerame Tuman. The other reason I felt everything was going our way stemmed from my ongoing affair with superstition. Every Thursday during the season, Joyce Price would bring me a pumpkin pie while watching film. That didn't happen in preparation for the Rose Bowl because we weren't in Pullman. The night before the game, right at bed check, there was a knock on my door. When I opened it, there was Joyce standing there with a pumpkin pie and Mike holding a glass of milk. "You didn't forget me!" I exclaimed, and tears started pouring down my face as I gave her a big hug. The pie made everything complete as far as I was concerned.

After weeks of hype and hoopla, we were more than ready to play come game day. With a police escort leading the way, our buses pulled into the Rose Bowl parking lot about four hours before the 2 p.m. kickoff. There in front of us was a mass of crimson and gray. The Cougar Nation had traveled well and now they were having the tailgate of a lifetime.

When we walked into the locker room, we were greeted by jerseys with Rose Bowl emblems on both shoulders and helmets with a rose and stem intertwined with the scripted Cougars logo. People had been waiting 67 years to see us step on the field looking like that. When I did go out onto the field, I remember looking down at the opposite end of the stadium and just barely making out the inscription in the end zone: WASHINGTON STATE. I don't know if I had ever run that fast in my life, but I took off on a dead sprint to get down there, to feel it, to make sure it was real.

After looking at the super-imposed "Washington State" Rose Bowl picture in the locker room for the last three years, and to finally see it become a reality on this sunny day, was like living a dream. To actually be on the field, to look up and see a blimp overhead, and to know that I was playing in a game that warranted a blimp, was nothing short of amazing to me. I wasn't the only one taking notice, When Mike Levenseller saw it he turned to Larry Lewis, our outstanding defensive ends coach and assistant head coach, and said, "We made it." Coaching in a blimp game, Levy explained, meant they had truly arrived.

As I walked back to the locker room, Coach Price pulled me aside. He made a few references about the game plan, and then looked at me and said, "Ryan, I would like you to join Dorian

(Boose) and Cory (Withrow) as captains for this ballgame. You deserve it. You have earned it." In those days, our captains were selected for each week's game rather than for the entire season. I had never been voted a captain, ever. In '96, I think it was because I wasn't everybody's favorite. And in '97, I was still a junior, and we had 26 very deserving seniors on the team. The quarterback on any team is a leader by definition, but the fact I'd never been voted a captain really bothered me. To be asked by the coach to do that in the biggest game of his career was such an honor, but Coach Price made it clear that it was the seniors who made the call – and that was the biggest honor of all.

When the team came running out of the tunnel before kickoff, you could just feel the Cougar pride in the air as our fans started cheering. I was already on the field, so I had the chance to view the team running out, and the fans' reaction, simultaneously. If you could freeze that moment, you'd have the perfect definition for the phrase "school spirit." I'm convinced two-thirds of that stadium was wearing crimson. They were loud and rowdy and proud. I could hear it in their voices and it just sent a jolt through me. It was a gorgeous day, New Year's Day, and the Washington State Cougars were in Pasadena to play the Michigan Wolverines. I spent four years aspiring to this day and just wanted to drink the place in to convince myself I was really here. It wasn't until years later that I would truly realize how important that day was to our thousands of fans in the stadium as well as the hundreds of thousands watching or listening at home.

Carol Burnett, the famous comedian, was the master of ceremonies for the Rose Parade, and that made her the designated coin flipper at midfield. She tossed the coin so hard it flew over the tops of the Michigan players and landed behind them. Michigan's quarterback was Brian Griese, a former walk-on and the son of hall-of-famer Bob Griese. He had a tremendous game that day and then went on to a long career in the NFL. The two of us, along with Charles Woodson and the Fab Five, were really kind of the toasts of the town in all the media coverage leading up to the game. Little did anyone know at the time but a guy who would go on to become one of the best players in the history of the NFL was warming the bench that day for Michigan – a sophomore no one had heard of by the name of Tom Brady. I don't even remember seeing him in warm ups that day. Of course, that shouldn't be surprising, because the only guy I was on the lookout for was Woodson. Michigan had a tremendous defense, an attacking, high-pressure defense featuring many future NFL players. Woodson, though, was just something else altogether. Their defensive coordinator, Brady Hoke – now the head coach of the Wolverines – would use him in a variety of ways that kept you off balance. I wasn't necessarily afraid of what he could do against our wide receivers as I was the angles he'd be coming in from on blitzes. Still, I was calm as a lake in Montana during this game. I had the standard nerves you get before any game, but that was it. I really felt like this was where I belonged, that I was born to be here. My lack of jitters wasn't shared by the Fab Five. Those guys were wired, and ended up dropping a number of first-half passes that they normally wouldn't have. They were coming into the huddle telling me who was open on the previous play. That had rarely happened during the regular season, when all I heard was, "Ryan, I'm open, I'm open." It was clear that it was going to take some time to get in full stride, but get this: Even with those uncharacteristic nerves, we still moved the ball up and down the field.

Twelve minutes into the first quarter, we scored – thanks in no small part to our punter, Jeff Banks, a senior who had come to WSU the year before after two seasons of junior college ball. Jeff was a good friend, my academic wing man in the Murrow School, and a heck of a good punter. He had pinned the Wolverines at their goal line after one of our drives had stalled around midfield. When Michigan's offense went nowhere, they punted and we got the ball back with a short field to work with. We drove down to their 15 and went into shotgun formation on a play with all kinds of passing options. Their middle linebacker went to cover Shawn Tims on an out route, leaving Kevin McKenzie open across the middle at about the goal line. Cougars 7, Wolverines 0! The WSU side of the field erupted. I sprinted to the sidelines like a little kid heading to the tree on Christmas morning. We had just gone 47 yards on six plays against the No. 1 defense in the country. This day was shaping up fine.

But it wasn't. Michael Black, our star running back, was a decoy on that play and hurt his right calf at about the time Kevin was stepping into the end zone. It was a fluky thing. Michael hadn't even been hit. He was just swinging out of the backfield and came down wrong on his leg. He thought trainers could massage out the problem, and he came back into the game for one carry on our next series. He gained no yards. He couldn't run. It was a nerve injury in the calf and he was done for the day. This was shattering, because Michael was no ordinary back. He was one of the best in the country. He piled up nearly 1,200 yards for us in 1997 and had an uncanny knack for making something big happen at exactly the right time. I got most of the headlines and the Heisman attention that season but Michael, in my eyes, was the MVP of the offense. Anytime things weren't clicking, we could hand the ball to him and he would keep us moving. Opposing defenses couldn't commit to stopping our passing game because Michael and the Fat Five would punish them up on the ground. If they committed to stopping the run, we'd shred them through the air. It was a perfect marriage. And now he was gone for the day, turning our offense one-dimensional. I remember Keith Jackson, talking about the game a few years later, saying we'd have "whopped 'em if Michael Black hadn't been injured." That was no insult to DeJuan Gilmore and Jayson Clayton, who subbed in for Michael. It was an acknowledgement of how talented Michael was, and how critical he was to the magic of 1997.

Overcoming challenges was something we had prided ourselves on, and Michael's injury just meant we all had to do a little more. The Cougar defense was playing another great game, and got us the ball back early in the second quarter. We proceeded to drive 63 yards – with Chris Jackson accounting for 35 of them on a nifty catch-and-run to the Michigan 14. In a play that I can still picture vividly, I was being grabbed by a Michigan lineman when I saw Shawn McWashington cutting across the back of the end zone. I laid a little finesse pass over the top. When I let go, I could tell I put too much on it. Shawn made an unbelievable, leaping effort to get to the ball. It was maybe an inch too far, and grazed his fingertips. We were that close to holding a 14-0 lead – a lead that I believe would have won us the game. DeJuan Gilmore carried the ball for two yards on the next play and then it was time to try the end zone again. I rolled left, looking to hit Kevin on a corner route. The ball got away from me a bit and fluttered short. It was still catchable, but not with Charles Woodson in the neighborhood. The guy must have jumped close to four feet off the ground. He leaped as high as I've ever seen any human leap and intercepted the ball. The complexion of the game was irrevocably changed at that point. Michigan subsequently went long, from Griese to Tai Streets to tie the game at 7, and that's where we ended up at halftime.

The third quarter was more of the same. We scored first, on a 14-yard reverse by Shawn Tims that capped a nine-play-99-yard drive that showed the world just how fabulous the Fab Five were. Besides Shawn's heroics, the drive included three passing plays of between 19 and 29 yards to McWashington, Jackson and McKenzie. Ninety-nine yards. That was a statement we had just made, the kind that can break the opposing team. Michigan didn't break. The Wolverines responded 20 seconds later with another bomb from Griese to Streets and they took the lead 14-13 (the PAT on our TD had been blocked).

Early in the fourth quarter, the Wolverines scored again, going up 21-13. They did it on a 14-play drive that covered 77 yards and a clock-draining five minutes and 29 seconds. It really was a beautiful piece of work – a classic example of Big Ten football. We answered with our own little drive, eight plays and 49 yards – 42 of it coming on a nice Gilmore reception – and then had to settle for a field goal. Rian Lindell, our walk-on sophomore kicker from Vancouver, Wash., drilled a beauty from 48-yards out. The pressure on him had been huge because a miss would have put every ounce of momentum on the other side. With the make, we were down 21-16 with a little more than seven minutes left to play. Plenty of time to give the Cougar Nation what they paid to see.

The Wolverines had other ideas, mounting another clock-sapping drive. Our defense had them in what seemed to be one third-and-long situation after another, and they kept making the first down by a half yard. Dorian Boose, Shane Doyle, Leon Bender and Gary Holmes all seemed to be within a whisker of sacking Griese time and again. He would be in the grasp, and then, wham, he was out. As I stood there on the sideline watching this happen, I was just in awe of the fact that they were doing this to our defense because our guys were good – really good – and our coordinator, Bill Doba, was a master tactician. I wanted to control the outcome of this game and Michigan's offense wasn't going to let me. This was excruciating to watch. Finally, inside a minute to go in the game, they hit fourth down and wound up pooch punting, but the damage was done. There were only 29 seconds left in the game, and we were getting the ball on our own seven with no timeouts left. The sun had just gone down, literally and figuratively.

When we broke the huddle on that first play, I honestly don't think there was any doubt among the 11 of us that we were going to take this the distance. Ninety-three yards in 29 seconds. It only takes one play, one series to get the ball in the end zone. That had been our battle cry all season. It wasn't going to change now. We were going to make history, right here and now, in front of a national television audience and 65,000 Cougars standing on their feet in Pasadena. First down. . . nothing. Second down. . . nothing.

258

Third down. . . a Hail Mary to Nian Taylor, jousting with Woodson down the right sideline, and a 46-yard gain. Nian had the savvy to get out of bounds to stop the clock and suddenly pulses started to race all over the stadium. By God, we were going to punch this thing in. The next play was one we had practiced for this exact, desperate kind of situation. The old truck-and-trailer, or hook-and-ladder. I hit Love Jefferson right in the numbers and then he smooth-as-silk tossed it to running back Jason Clayton for a 26-yard gain. Clock stopped, at two seconds, to reset the chains. Ball at the Michigan 26. Twenty-six yards to history, 26 yards to one of the greatest endings ever. We had come here to defeat the No. 1 team in the nation, and we were going to do just that.

We scrambled up to the line and got set. The whistle blew to signal the clock start and Lee Harrison fired the ball into my hands. I spiked it. I looked at the clock after the ball left my hand and it said one second. Yet the clock continued to run down to zero. Then there was another whistle, and I looked over to the official and saw him waving his hands, signaling the end of the game. Michigan players stormed onto the field, while our side and our fans looked on stunned, knowing we had one more play . . . waiting for the right call to be made. It never came. I about lost it. I ran after the official and told him in no uncertain terms that this was wrong. We had another snap coming to us. In what must have been a world-record sprint for a 50-year-old who liked to barbeque far more than exercise, Coach Price grabbed me, gave me a hug and whispered in my ear, "Don't say anything. Don't talk about the two seconds at all. Let me deal with it. You be gracious. You played your heart out. You willed us this whole season. Let me deal with it."

His words registered. There was nothing we could do at this point. There was no use making a scene. This was about bigger things. This was about Washington State and how we handled ourselves all season. We weren't going to cry over the controversy, we were going to get over this disappointment and rejoice in a season no one would ever forget. The controversial end just added to the intrigue of it all. We didn't lose, we just ran out of time, as the next day's Spokesman-Review said. The newspaper ran a huge headline on the front page that read "But What a Game." With it was a picture of me and Coach Price, arm in arm, walking off the field. A short editorial appeared beneath it.

> *"The Cougars awed and impressed those both near and far. Even naysayers found renewed faith in watching athletes who saw success in playing hard and playing fair. There's something to be said for teamwork, for pride and for believing, if only for a moment, in a collective identity borne of big dreams and long-shot hopes. Washington State offered us that moment this year. May the words "Go Cougs" continue to inspire and motivate us long after Jan. 1, 1998."*

There was no name on those words. It couldn't have been written any better by Coach Price. Those words captured the essence of our 1997 Cougars. We were a collection of characters, some from the sticks and some from the big city. We were white and black, big and small, quiet and loud and everything in between. Above all, we were committed and loyal and determined.

As I walked off the field with Coach Price, I looked to the stands and all our fans were still there. I don't think a one of them left. They were on their feet clapping and cheering. We had just lost a real battle. They were bummed out and we were crestfallen, yet the broader picture – this long, glorious journey – was why they were on their feet. I started blowing kisses to them and shouting "thank you." This would be my final walk in a Cougar uniform. I'd told my teammates a couple of days before that I was going to declare for the NFL draft, and I would make it official at a news conference the next day with Coach Price at my side.

Amid all this I had forgotten something important. I was already up the tunnel when I realized my oversight, so I ran back out to the field and found my mom in the stands with tears in her eyes. We gave each other the biggest, tightest hug and held on for a long time, knowing that this was the end of four very special years for both us and our entire family.

Entering that locker room was tough. This amazing ride together was over, and it hadn't ended the way it was supposed to. We cried and hugged. Other than Jason McEndoo and Ryan McShane, it was the most emotional I'd ever seen any of the guys on the team. These big, strong football players were heartbroken. In the post-game media briefing, I sat with Leon, Dorian and Shawn. They were complimentary of Michigan, who had held us 33 points below our per-game average. They expressed how much their teammates meant to them. And they said they hoped what we had accomplished would launch a new chapter in Washington State football – a hope we saw come to true when Jason Gesser led the Cougars to the Rose Bowl five years later and Matt Kegel guided them to a victory over Vince Young and No. 5 Texas in the

Holiday Bowl a year after that.

"We were only mid-fabulous today on the fabulous meter," Shawn said of his amazing Five. Leon said he'd never get over the loss. "I think it will still be a big issue when I'm 80. We worked so hard to get here, and to lose the game the way we did really hurt. If we would have lost by two touchdowns, it would have been easier to accept." Ray Jackson had perhaps the most colorful summary, saying he had "an empty feeling, like somebody stole your bike or ice cream cone."

To this day, I haven't had the heart to sit down and watch the game on tape. My dad saw it on ESPN Classic one time and said I probably shouldn't watch. I would be too upset, especially with the technology nowadays that shows to the tenth how many seconds are on the clock.

Who's to know if we would have scored on that would-be final play. Twenty-six yards is no short distance in a football game. With five great receivers and a proven play ready to run, you just never know. Michigan coach Lloyd Carr said "I knew anything was possible with Ryan Leaf in the game." I appreciated the compliment, but would have rather had the chance. The "What could have been?" aspect to it still sneaks into my thoughts every once in a great while. When I went to bed that night, however, I knew our team had put heart and soul into every snap of the game. There were no regrets.

The next morning I held my press conference announcing my NFL plans. The place was packed with reporters and TV cameras. Coach Price spoke first. He talked glowingly and lovingly about me. The feeling, of course, was mutual. And I actually started to second-guess myself for a moment right there in the room. I looked at my mom and dad. Both of them wanted me to stay at WSU, especially my mom, who truly knew how immature I still was. My mother knows me emotionally. My father was more practical. He knew the Cougars would struggle the next season because so many seniors were leaving. He knew my draft stock couldn't go any higher than it was, and that injury was always a risk in football. So from that standpoint, he completely understood why I wanted to start my NFL dream. He still wanted me to return to WSU though.

All these years later, with the clarity of hindsight, my parents were so right. Going to the NFL when I did was absolutely the wrong decision. I wasn't ready mentally or emotionally. Returning to the Cougars in 1998 would have been a tremendous life lesson in battling adversity, and in having to be THE team leader because the Withrows and McEndoos and Booses and Benders were gone. I also think I could have helped that team win enough games to get to a bowl. Yet, I had my mind set. It was an ego thing. I wanted to be the top pick in the draft, and I wanted to come out a year early to show people how good I was.

As I got up and gave my speech and thanked Washington State University, and the fans, and Coach Price, and my parents, I had this urge to flip it all around. I had this urge to say, "I just can't do it. I'm coming back. I'm gonna be a Cougar again." I dream about that, and I dream about me saying those words and my life turning out differently. But I didn't. I was at the precipice of my dream, and all I had to say was, "I'm moving on. I'm taking the next challenge. I'm going to be an NFL quarterback." That's what I did.

On that day – January 2, 1998 – I walked away from a great

year of my life into an unknown abyss that would ultimately gobble me up. What I didn't realize at the time is how life-affirmingly-special that season was, not only to me, but to everyone associated with Washington State, from the administration to the coaching staff and players to our fans and their kids, the future Cougars.

For too long, I had forgotten the lessons of loyalty, friendship, and perseverance that I learned at Washington State. I ran from my past because I felt I'd let everyone down in my professional career. If only I had run to it. The Cougar Nation is embracing. It's about spirit and community. When grown men come up to me with moist eyes and say "thank you" for 1997, I wonder how I could have been so clueless to think Cougars would turn their backs on me because of what happened in San Diego. There's not a day that goes by that I don't thank God for the phone call I received on January 1, 1994 from Mike Price asking me if I wanted to play for Washington State and go to the Rose Bowl together. I believed him, and we did. We did what many people thought was impossible. The blueprint was unique, the people – on and off the field – were unforgettable, and the ride – that joyous ride – binds us forever.

INDEX